Exploring Wiccan Ethics

Ethical Enchantments: Nurturing the Soul with Wiccan Philosophy and Ethical Practices

Emily Greene

Table of Contents

INTRODUCTION

Welcome to "Exploring Wiccan Ethics: Ethical Enchantments - Nurturing the Soul with Wiccan Philosophy and Ethical Practices." Within these pages, we embark on a profound journey into the heart of Wicca, a spiritual path that honors nature, celebrates life cycles, and embraces ethical principles as its guiding light.

Wicca, often misunderstood and mysterious, is a modern pagan tradition rooted in ancient wisdom. It offers a tapestry of beliefs, rituals, and ethical codes that empower individuals to explore their spirituality and live in harmony with the world around them. This ebook is your key to unlocking the mysteries of Wiccan philosophy and ethics, delving deep into its core tenets, practices, and ethical considerations.

In the following chapters, we will explore the foundations of Wicca, its reverence for the natural world, and the profound interconnectedness it recognizes among all living beings. We will delve into the ethical compass that guides Wiccans in their daily lives and magical endeavors, shedding light on the often-misunderstood concepts of the Wiccan Rede and the Threefold Law.

Moreover, we will uncover the art of crafting ethical enchantments through spells and rituals that transform the outer world and nourish the inner self. We will discuss the role of meditation, mindfulness, and personal growth in Wiccan practice and how these elements contribute to nurturing the soul.

Throughout this journey, we will also examine the intersection of Wiccan ethics with social responsibility, the challenges Wiccans face in a diverse world, and strategies for authentic Wiccan life.

Whether you are a seasoned practitioner seeking to deepen your understanding or a newcomer curious about Wicca's profound philosophy, this ebook is your guide to exploring this ancient yet ever-relevant path's magic, ethics, and spirituality. So, let us embark together on this enchanting voyage into the heart and soul of Wiccan philosophy and ethics.

CHAPTER I

Wicca as a Spiritual Path

History and origins of Wicca

Wicca, often called modern witchcraft, is a contemporary pagan, nature-based religious movement that has gained popularity and visibility over the past century. Its history and origins are a fascinating blend of ancient traditions, folklore, and the creative innovations of 20th-century figures. This section will delve into the complex tapestry of Wicca's historical development and its emergence as a distinct spiritual path.

The roots of Wicca can be traced back to pre-Christian pagan traditions, particularly those of Western Europe. These ancient belief systems revered nature, recognized the cycles of the seasons, and practiced various forms of magic. Elements of these pagan practices and beliefs served as foundational concepts upon which Wicca would later be built.

One significant influence on the development of Wicca was the resurgence of interest in Western occultism in the late 19th and early 20th centuries. Figures like Aleister Crowley and the Hermetic Order of the Golden Dawn popularized ideas about mysticism, ritual magic, and the esoteric. These influences would later find their way into the evolving framework of Wiccan practice.

However, in the mid-20th century, Wicca began to take its modern form. One of the most prominent figures in this process was Gerald Gardner, a retired British civil servant interested in the occult. Gardner claimed to have been initiated into a witchcraft tradition by a New Forest coven, and he went on to write about his experiences and beliefs in books such as "Witchcraft Today" (1954) and "The Meaning of Witchcraft" (1959).

Gardner's writings and public appearances brought witchcraft into the public eye, and he is often referred to as the "Father of Wicca." He presented Wicca as a contemporary, nature-focused, and witchcraft-centered religion, emphasizing the worship of a Goddess and God, the observance of seasonal festivals (the Sabbats), and the practice of magic. Gardnerian Wicca, as his tradition came to be known, became one of the earliest and most influential branches of modern witchcraft.

Another key figure in the history of Wicca is Doreen Valiente, a high priestess in Gardnerian Wicca who played a crucial role in refining and expanding Wiccan rituals and practices. Valiente contributed significantly to the Book of Shadows, a sacred text in Wicca containing rituals, spells, and ethical guidelines. Her influence helped shape Wicca's spiritual and magical aspects, making it more accessible to a broader audience.

As Wicca continued to evolve, other traditions and offshoots emerged. One such tradition is Alexandrian Wicca, founded by Alex Sanders and his wife, Maxine Sanders, in the 1960s. Alexandrian Wicca shared some similarities with Gardnerian Wicca but incorporated additional elements, such as a stronger focus on ceremonial magic.

The spread of Wicca to the United States and other parts of the world in the mid-20th century was facilitated by authors like Raymond Buckland and Scott Cunningham, who wrote books that introduced Wiccan concepts and practices to a broader audience. This globalization of Wicca contributed to its diversification, with practitioners adapting it to their cultural contexts and personal beliefs.

Despite its relatively short history compared to ancient religions, Wicca has continued to evolve and thrive into the 21st century. There are now numerous Wiccan traditions and eclectic forms of witchcraft, each with its unique practices and interpretations of Wiccan principles. Wicca has also gained recognition as a legitimate religious path in many countries, leading to legal protections for Wiccan practitioners.

In conclusion, the history and origins of Wicca are a blend of ancient pagan traditions, Western occultism, and the creative contributions of 20th-century figures like Gerald Gardner and Doreen Valiente. Wicca's emergence as a modern pagan religion with a focus on nature, magic, and the worship of a Goddess and God has made it a diverse and vibrant spiritual movement. Its history reflects the human capacity for spiritual innovation and adaptation, drawing from both ancient wisdom and contemporary insights to create a unique and enduring path. As Wicca continues to evolve, it remains a testament to the lasting fascination with the mysteries of nature and the magic of the human spirit.

Core beliefs and principles of Wicca

Wicca, a contemporary pagan and nature-based religion, is characterized by a set of core beliefs and principles that form the foundation of its spiritual practices and worldview. Often misunderstood or misrepresented, Wicca strongly emphasizes harmony with nature, reverence for the divine, and ethical conduct. In this section, we will explore these core beliefs and principles in detail, shedding light on the essence of Wiccan spirituality.

Central to Wicca is the veneration of nature as sacred. Wiccans view the natural world as a manifestation of divine energy, where every element, plant, and creature possesses inherent value and significance. This reverence for nature is deeply rooted in ancient pagan traditions, where the cycles of the seasons, the phases of the moon, and the changing tides held spiritual significance. Wiccans celebrate and align their rituals with these natural rhythms, recognizing the interconnectedness of all life and the importance of living in harmony with the Earth.

The concept of polarity is another fundamental belief in Wicca. Wiccans often perceive the divine as a duality—a Goddess and God, often representing feminine and masculine energies. These deities are seen as complementary forces, embodying various aspects of existence. The Goddess symbolizes fertility, nurturing, and the cycles of birth, growth, and death, while the God represents strength, protection, and the cycles of the seasons. The interplay of these dualities is central to Wiccan rituals and magical workings, where balance and harmony are sought.

Wiccan worship occurs within a sacred circle, a symbolic representation of the protective boundary between the mundane and the sacred. The circle is believed to create a space where the divine energies can be accessed and manipulated. This concept is linked to the principle of magic in Wicca, which is the art of channeling and directing these energies to create change or transformation. Magic is seen as a natural and ethical practice, and Wiccans adhere to a code of ethics when using magical techniques.

Perhaps one of Wicca's most well-known ethical guidelines is the Wiccan Rede, which states, "An it harm none, do what ye will." This succinct maxim emphasizes the importance of responsible and ethical behavior. It encourages Wiccans to consider the potential consequences of their actions and strive for actions that cause no harm to others or themselves. While it may seem simple, the Wiccan Rede is a powerful reminder of the interconnectedness of all life and the responsibility that comes with wielding magical power.

The Threefold Law is closely related to the Wiccan Rede, often summarized as "Whatever you send out into the universe, it will return to you threefold." This concept reinforces the idea of karma or cause and effect, suggesting that the consequences of one's actions will come back amplified. This belief serves as a moral compass for Wiccans, guiding them to act with mindfulness and integrity in all aspects of life, magical or otherwise.

The Wheel of the Year is a central component of Wiccan practice, representing the annual cycle of seasons and the corresponding festivals or Sabbats. There are eight Sabbats in total, divided into two categories: the Lesser Sabbats, which mark the solstices and equinoxes, and the Greater Sabbats, which celebrate the cross-quarter days between the solstices and equinoxes. These festivals provide opportunities for Wiccans to connect with the energies of the seasons, celebrate the cycles of life and death, and express gratitude for the Earth's bounty. Ritual and symbolism play a significant role in Wiccan practice. Wiccans perform rituals within their sacred circles, invoking the divine, working magic, and honoring the cycles of nature. Symbolism is abundant in Wiccan rituals, with tools like the athame (ritual knife), chalice, wand, and pentacle representing various elements and aspects of the divine. Candles, incense, and herbs are used to enhance the atmosphere and raise energy during rituals.

The Book of Shadows is a key component of Wiccan practice, serving as a personal and/or coven-specific guidebook containing rituals, spells, and records of magical work. It is a dynamic and evolving document that reflects the practitioner's spiritual journey and experiences. The Book of Shadows is a repository of knowledge, tradition, and personal insights, often passed down through generations within a coven or shared among solitary practitioners.

Covens, groups of Wiccans who gather for worship and magical work, are a common feature of Wiccan practice, but not all Wiccans belong to covens. Some prefer to practice as solitaries, following their own path and rituals. Covens provide a supportive community where members can learn, grow, and share their spiritual experiences, but they also come with responsibilities, such as adherence to group rituals and ethical guidelines.

In conclusion, Wicca's core beliefs and principles form a rich and multifaceted tapestry that emphasizes harmony with nature, reverence for the divine, and ethical conduct. These beliefs are deeply intertwined with the practice of magic, rituals, and celebrating the Wheel of the Year. Wicca is a modern, adaptable, and diverse spiritual path that draws from ancient traditions while embracing contemporary insights and individual interpretations. Ultimately, at the heart of Wiccan spirituality is a profound connection to the natural world and a commitment to living in balance and harmony with it, guided by a strong code of ethics and respect for all living beings.

Different traditions within Wicca

Wicca, a contemporary pagan and nature-based religion, is not a monolithic belief system but rather a diverse tapestry of traditions and practices. While all Wiccans share some core beliefs and principles, such as reverence for nature and a focus on magic, there is significant variation in how these beliefs are interpreted and applied. This section will explore some of the different traditions within Wicca, highlighting their unique characteristics and contributions to the broader Wiccan community.

One of Wicca's earliest and most well-known traditions is Gardnerian Wicca, founded by Gerald Gardner in the mid-20th century. Gardnerian Wicca is often considered the archetype of Wiccan traditions and has profoundly influenced the development of modern witchcraft. It emphasizes the worship of a Goddess and God, the use of ceremonial tools, and adherence to a specific initiation process. Gardnerian covens, organized groups of Wiccans, follow a hierarchical structure and a Book of Shadows that contains their rituals and teachings.

Alexandrian Wicca, founded by Alex Sanders in the 1960s, is closely related to Gardnerian Wicca and shares many of its core practices. However, Alexandrian Wicca emphasizes ceremonial magic, incorporating elements from the Hermetic Order of the Golden Dawn and the Qabalah. This tradition is known for its eclectic approach, which allows practitioners to incorporate diverse influences into their magical and ritual work.

Dianic Wicca, also known as Dianic Witchcraft, is a tradition that strongly emphasizes the Goddess and often excludes or downplays the worship of a God. This tradition is often associated with feminist spirituality and celebrates the divine feminine in all its forms. Dianic covens vary in their practices, but many focus on women's empowerment, healing, and social activism. Some Dianic groups are exclusively for women, while others are open to all genders.

Eclectic Wicca is a flexible and adaptable tradition that draws from various sources and practices. Eclectic Wiccans often create their unique blend of rituals, beliefs, and magical techniques, incorporating elements from different Wiccan traditions as well as other spiritual paths. This eclecticism allows practitioners to tailor their practice to their individual preferences and needs. Eclectic Wicca is a popular choice for solitaries, those who practice Wicca on their own, as it provides a framework that can be personalized.

Traditional British Witchcraft, often referred to as Traditional Witchcraft or simply "the Craft," predates the emergence of Wicca as a distinct religious tradition. It draws from folk magic, herbalism, and regional witchcraft practices found in the British Isles. Traditional Witches typically work with the land, spirits of place, and local folklore. Unlike Wicca, which has a more standardized structure, Traditional Witchcraft is highly diverse and decentralized, with individual practitioners and covens following their unique traditions.

Seax-Wicca is a tradition founded by Raymond Buckland in the 1970s that draws inspiration from both Wicca and the folk magic practices of the Anglo-Saxons. It strongly emphasizes self-initiation and is known for its practical approach to magic, often utilizing everyday objects and tools. Seax-Wicca is characterized by its simplicity and accessibility, making it an attractive choice for beginners and solitary practitioners.

Feri Tradition, founded by Victor and Cora Anderson in the mid-20th century, is a unique and enigmatic tradition in modern witchcraft. Feri emphasizes personal gnosis, direct mystical experiences, and the development of psychic abilities. It draws from various spiritual influences, including European witchcraft, Gnosticism, and African and African-American folklore. Feri is known for its emphasis on ecstatic and trance-based practices.

The Covenant of the Goddess (CoG) is not a specific Wiccan tradition but an umbrella organization representing a diverse group of Wiccan covens and practitioners. CoG is dedicated to promoting religious freedom, ethical conduct, and cooperation within the Wiccan community. It offers a platform for networking as well as collaboration among Wiccan traditions and serves as an advocacy group for Wiccan rights and recognition.

In conclusion, Wicca is a multifaceted and diverse religion with a rich tapestry of traditions, each offering its unique approach to spirituality, magic, and ritual. While all Wiccans share common values and principles, the diversity of Wiccan traditions reflects the adaptability and creativity of its practitioners. Whether one is drawn to the structure of Gardnerian Wicca, the feminist focus of Dianic Wicca, the eclectic freedom of Eclectic Wicca, or the rich folklore of Traditional Witchcraft, there is a Wiccan tradition to suit a wide range of spiritual needs and preferences. This diversity is a testament to the vitality and resilience of the Wiccan community, which continues to evolve and thrive in the modern world.

Notable figures in Wiccan history

Wicca, a contemporary pagan and nature-based religion, has a relatively short but rich history that spans just a few decades. During this time, several notable figures have shaped and popularized Wiccan beliefs, practices, and traditions. In this section, we will explore the lives and contributions of some of these key figures, shedding light on their significant influence on the development of modern witchcraft.

One of the central figures in the history of Wicca is Gerald Gardner (1884-1964), often referred to as the "Father of Wicca." Gardner was a British civil servant as well as an amateur anthropologist who is credited with bringing Wicca into the public eye in the mid-20th century. He claimed to have been initiated into a witchcraft tradition in the New Forest region of England and went on to write several books, such as "Witchcraft Today" (1954) and "The Meaning of Witchcraft" (1959), in which he shared his experiences and beliefs. Gardner's writings and public appearances played a pivotal role in the popularization of witchcraft, and his tradition, known as Gardnerian Wicca, became one of the earliest and most influential branches of modern witchcraft.

Doreen Valiente (1922-1999) is another significant figure in the history of Wicca and is often referred to as the "Mother of Modern Witchcraft." Valiente, a high priestess in Gardnerian Wicca, made substantial contributions to the refinement and expansion of Wiccan rituals and practices. She worked closely with Gardner to edit and augment the Book of Shadows, a sacred text in Wicca containing rituals, spells, and ethical guidelines. Valiente's influence helped shape Wicca's spiritual and magical aspects, making it more accessible and inclusive. Her dedication to preserving and promoting the Craft's spiritual and ethical dimensions continues to inspire contemporary Wiccans.

Raymond Buckland (1934-2017) was a prolific author and practitioner who was crucial in introducing Wicca to a broader audience, particularly in the United States. Originally from England, Buckland moved to the United States in the 1960s and became one of the first individuals to teach and write about Wicca publicly in the country. His books, including "Witchcraft from the Inside" (1971) and "Complete Book of Witchcraft" (1986), helped demystify Wicca and provided practical guidance for those interested in its practices. Buckland's work contributed significantly to the growth of Wiccan communities in the United States and helped dispel misconceptions about witchcraft.

Scott Cunningham (1956-1993) was another influential author and Wiccan practitioner known for his accessible and beginner-friendly approach to Wicca. His books, such as "Wicca: A Guide for the Solitary Practitioner" (1988) and "Living Wicca: A Further Guide for the Solitary Practitioner" (1993), provided a clear and practical introduction to Wiccan beliefs and practices. Cunningham's emphasis on self-initiation and solitary practice resonated with many newcomers to Wicca and helped foster a sense of empowerment and independence among solitary practitioners.

Zsuzsanna Budapest is a notable figure in the history of Dianic Wicca, a feminist and Goddess-centered tradition within Wicca. Budapest, a Hungarian-born American, founded the Susan B. Anthony Coven No. 1 in Los Angeles in the 1970s, which is considered one of the earliest Dianic Wiccan covens. Her book "The Holy Book of Women's Mysteries" (1979) and her advocacy for women's spirituality and empowerment have impacted the feminist spirituality movement. Budapest's work highlights the importance of the divine feminine in Wiccan and pagan traditions and underscores the role of activism and social change within spirituality.

Alex Sanders (1926-1988) was a British occultist and the founder of Alexandrian Wicca, a tradition closely related to Gardnerian Wicca. Sanders and his wife, Maxine Sanders, played a significant role in developing and popularizing this tradition in the 1960s. Alexandrian Wicca incorporated ceremonial magic elements and placed a strong emphasis on the role of the priestess in ritual. The Sanders' work helped expand the diversity of Wiccan traditions and introduced new magical techniques and approaches.

Starhawk, a pen name for Miriam Simos, is a prominent figure in the modern witchcraft and feminist spirituality movements. Her book "The Spiral Dance: A Rebirth of the Ancient Religion of the Great Goddess" (1979) is considered a seminal work in contemporary Wiccan literature. Starhawk's writings focus on eco-spirituality, social justice, and the importance of environmental stewardship. She is also known for her activism and advocacy for a more sustainable and equitable world, reflecting the ethical dimensions of Wiccan spirituality.

In conclusion, these notable figures have made indelible contributions to the development, popularization, and diversification of Wicca and modern witchcraft. Their writings, teachings, and advocacy efforts have helped shape the practice of Wicca and have inspired countless individuals to explore its spiritual dimensions. While the history of Wicca is relatively brief, the influence of these figures continues to resonate within the global Wiccan community, reminding us of the enduring relevance and adaptability of this nature-based religion.

Modern expressions and variations of Wicca

Wicca, a modern pagan and nature-based religious tradition, has evolved and diversified significantly since its emergence in the mid-20th century. While rooted in a set of core beliefs and principles, modern Wicca has given rise to various expressions, traditions, and variations. In this section, we will explore the contemporary expressions of Wicca, highlighting how this dynamic and adaptable spirituality has continued to grow and evolve.

One of the most significant developments in modern Wicca is the proliferation of different traditions and lineages. While Gardnerian and Alexandrian Wicca were the earliest and most influential traditions, many others have emerged since. These include Dianic Wicca, Seax-Wicca, Eclectic Wicca, Traditional Witchcraft, and more. Each tradition has its unique rituals, practices, and emphases, making Wicca a diverse and multifaceted spiritual path. These variations reflect the adaptability of Wicca and its capacity to evolve to meet the needs and preferences of practitioners.

Dianic Wicca, for instance, is a tradition that strongly emphasizes the divine feminine and often excludes or downplays the worship of a God. It has gained popularity as a feminist and women-centered expression of Wicca, focusing on women's empowerment, healing, and spirituality. Dianic covens vary in their practices, with some exclusively for women and others open to all genders. This tradition highlights the diversity of beliefs and practices within Wicca, as well as its capacity to respond to the unique spiritual requirements of different communities.

Seax-Wicca, founded by Raymond Buckland in the 1970s, incorporates Anglo-Saxon folk magic and spirituality elements. It emphasizes self-initiation and practical, accessible magical techniques, making it particularly appealing to newcomers and solitaries. Seax-Wicca's simplicity and adaptability have contributed to its popularity among modern practitioners seeking a down-to-earth and personalized approach to Wicca.

Eclectic Wicca is a flexible and adaptable expression of the tradition that draws from various sources and practices. Eclectic Wiccans often create their unique blend of rituals, beliefs, and magical techniques, incorporating elements from different Wiccan traditions and other spiritual paths. This eclecticism allows practitioners to tailor their practice to their individual preferences and needs, highlighting the personalization and autonomy that are integral to modern Wicca.

Traditional Witchcraft, sometimes simply called "the Craft," predates the emergence of Wicca as a distinct religious tradition. It draws from folk magic, herbalism, and regional witchcraft practices found in the British Isles. Traditional Witches typically work with the land, spirits of place, and local folklore. Unlike Wicca, which has a more standardized structure, Traditional Witchcraft is highly diverse and decentralized, with individual practitioners and covens following their unique traditions. This diversity reflects the rich tapestry of folk magical practices and beliefs that have contributed to the development of modern witchcraft.

The rise of solitary practitioners is another noteworthy development in modern Wicca. While covens, organized groups of Wiccans, have traditionally played an important role in the practice of Wicca, many individuals now choose to practice Wicca on their own. Solitary Wiccans often adapt rituals and practices to suit their individual preferences and schedules. This shift toward solitary practice reflects the growing autonomy and accessibility of Wicca, allowing individuals to explore and deepen their spirituality independently.

Moreover, the globalization of Wicca has led to the emergence of regional variations and adaptations of the tradition. Wicca has found adherents and practitioners in various parts of the world, each bringing their cultural perspectives and influences to the practice of Wicca. For example, British Traditional Wicca, often considered the root tradition, has evolved differently in the United States, creating American Traditional Wicca traditions with their unique rituals and practices. Similarly, Wicca practiced in Australia, South America, or Asia may incorporate elements of local spirituality, folklore, and mythology, enriching the global tapestry of Wiccan expressions.

The advent of the internet has also played a transformative role in modern Wicca. Online communities, forums, as well as social media platforms have provided a space for Wiccans worldwide to connect, share knowledge, and discuss their experiences. This virtual interconnectedness has allowed practitioners to learn from one another, exchange ideas, and access resources that were once limited to specific geographic regions or covens. It has promoted a sense of global community and collaboration among Wiccans, further diversifying and enriching the tradition.

In conclusion, modern expressions and variations of Wicca reflect its dynamic and adaptable nature. From the emergence of diverse traditions to the growth of solitary practice and the globalization of Wicca, this contemporary pagan tradition continues to evolve and respond to its practitioners' changing needs and preferences. The flexibility, diversity, and inclusivity of modern Wicca highlight its enduring appeal and its capacity to stay relevant and also vibrant in the 21st century.

CHAPTER II

The Foundations of Wiccan Philosophy

Exploring the concept of nature as sacred in Wicca

At the heart of Wicca, a contemporary pagan and nature-based religion, lies the profound concept of nature as sacred. This reverence for the natural world is a foundational belief that underpins the entire Wiccan spiritual framework. This section will delve into the multifaceted concept of nature as sacred in Wicca, exploring its significance, manifestations, and implications for Wiccan beliefs and practices.

One of the defining features of Wicca is its deep connection with the natural world. Wiccans view nature as sacred, not distant and untouchable, but as an immanent and vibrant force that surrounds and permeates their lives. In Wiccan belief, nature is not separate from humanity but is intricately intertwined with it. This view reflects the idea that the divine is immanent, present in all things, and that the physical world reflects the spiritual.

Recognizing the cycles of life, death, and rebirth is central to the concept of nature as sacred in Wicca. Wiccans celebrate the changing seasons and the waxing and waning of the moon as symbolic representations of these cycles. The Wheel of the Year, a series of eight festivals or Sabbats, marks the turning points in these cycles and provides opportunities for Wiccans to connect with the energies of nature. For example, the festival of Samhain, celebrated on October 31st, marks the end of the old year and the beginning of the new. It is a time to honor the ancestors and reflect on mortality and transformation.

Wiccans often perform rituals and ceremonies outdoors, in natural settings like forests, gardens, or meadows. This practice, known as "skyclad" or "naked" ritual, is intended to enhance the practitioner's connection with nature and the divine. By physically immersing themselves in the natural world, Wiccans seek to embody their belief in the sacredness of nature.

The elements—earth, air, fire, water, and spirit—are also integral to the concept of nature as sacred in Wicca. These elements are seen as fundamental building blocks of the universe and are revered in their own right. Wiccans work with the elements in rituals and magical practices, calling upon their energies and symbolism to create change and transformation. For example, water may be used for purification and emotional healing, while fire may be invoked for courage and energy.

The concept of a dual divinity—the God and Goddess—is another essential aspect of nature as sacred in Wicca. These deities are often associated with natural forces and elements. The Goddess is seen as the embodiment of the Earth and the cycles of nature, while the God represents the sun, the harvest, and the vitality of life. The interplay between these dualities reflects the cycles of growth, birth, death, and rebirth that are observed in the natural world. Wiccans celebrate the changing roles of the God and Goddess throughout the Wheel of the Year, honoring their respective attributes and powers.

Wiccans often refer to the Earth as "the Great Mother," emphasizing the nurturing and life-giving qualities associated with the feminine divine. This personification of the Earth highlights the interconnectedness of all life and the recognition that the Earth provides sustenance, shelter, and beauty. Many Wiccans view the Earth as sentient, deserving of respect and care. This perspective has led to a strong emphasis on environmentalism and eco-spirituality within the Wiccan community.

Ethical considerations also play an important role in the concept of nature as sacred in Wicca. The Wiccan Rede, a central ethical guideline in Wicca, states, "An it harm none, do what ye will." This principle emphasizes the importance of responsible and ethical behavior and highlights the interconnectedness of all life. Wiccans believe that harming others or the natural world ultimately harms oneself, as reflected in the concept of the Threefold Law, which suggests that the consequences of one's actions will return threefold.

Rituals and magical practices in Wicca often involve using natural materials such as herbs, crystals, and candles. These tools are believed to harness the energies of the natural world and the elements, making them powerful conduits for magic and spiritual connection. For example, the use of herbs in spellwork draws upon plants' healing and transformative properties, aligning the practitioner with the forces of nature.

Furthermore, the concept of nature as sacred in Wicca extends beyond the individual practitioner to the broader community and the world at large. Wiccans often engage in environmental activism and stewardship, seeking to protect and preserve the Earth's ecosystems. This commitment to environmental responsibility reflects the belief that humanity has a sacred duty to care for the Earth and its creatures.

In conclusion, the concept of nature as sacred in Wicca is a foundational and multifaceted belief that permeates every aspect of this contemporary pagan tradition. It encompasses the recognition of cycles, the reverence for the elements, the veneration of the God and Goddess, and ethical considerations that guide Wiccan behavior. This sacred connection to nature not only informs Wiccan rituals and practices but also inspires a deep sense of responsibility and care for the Earth and its ecosystems. Ultimately, in Wicca, nature is not only a source of inspiration and wonder but also a profound and enduring spiritual presence that calls upon its practitioners to live in harmony with the natural world.

The role of deity and the God/Goddess in Wiccan philosophy

Wicca, a contemporary pagan and nature-based religion, places a central focus on the concept of deity, often represented as a dual divinity—the God and Goddess. This divine duality is at the core of Wiccan philosophy and spirituality, shaping beliefs, practices, and the entire worldview of Wiccans. In this section, we will explore the role of deity and the God/Goddess in Wiccan philosophy, examining their significance, attributes, and influence on the Wiccan spiritual path.

The belief in a dual divinity—the God and Goddess—is one of the defining features of Wicca. This divine duality is often understood as a reflection of the complementary forces in nature, symbolizing the interplay of masculine and feminine energies. The Goddess is seen as the embodiment of the Earth, the moon, and the cycles of nature. She represents fertility, nurturing, and the mysteries of life, death, and rebirth. The God, conversely, is associated with the sun, the hunt, and the cycles of the seasons. He embodies strength, protection, and the vital force of life.

The dual divinity of the God and Goddess is not perceived as distant or transcendent but as inherent and present in all things. Wiccans believe that the divine can be encountered directly through a personal and intimate connection with the natural world. This belief is rooted in the idea that the physical world is a reflection of the spiritual, and that the Earth, in all its beauty and complexity, is sacred. This perspective informs Wiccan rituals, which often occur outdoors in natural settings, to enhance the practitioner's connection with nature and the divine.

Wiccans celebrate the changing roles and attributes of the God and Goddess throughout the Wheel of the Year, a series of eight festivals or Sabbats that mark the cycles of the seasons. Each festival is an opportunity to honor and connect with specific aspects of the divine. For example, the festival of Beltane, celebrated in May, is dedicated to the union of the God and Goddess, symbolizing the generative power of life and the vitality of nature. On the other hand, the festival of Yule, celebrated in December, honors God's rebirth and the sun's return after the darkest days of winter.

Rituals in Wicca often invoke the God and Goddess, calling upon their energies and symbolism to create change and transformation. These rituals may involve using sacred tools, such as the athame (ritual knife) or chalice, to channel and direct these energies. Casting a sacred circle, a symbolic boundary between the mundane and the sacred, is a common practice in Wiccan rituals. The divine presence is invoked within this circle, and magical work is performed.

The concept of deity in Wicca is not fixed or dogmatic but is open to individual interpretation and experience. Wiccans believe in a "soft polytheism," where the God and Goddess can take on various forms and aspects to suit the needs and perspectives of the practitioner. This fluidity allows Wiccans to relate to the divine in ways that resonate with their personal beliefs and experiences. Some Wiccans may work with specific deities from different pantheons, such as Celtic, Norse, or Egyptian, while others may perceive the God and Goddess as archetypal symbols rather than literal beings.

The dual divinity of the God and Goddess is often likened to the concept of the "Great Mother" and the "Horned God." The Great Mother represents the nurturing and life-giving aspect of the divine, embodying the Earth and its cycles. The Horned God represents the vital and protective aspects of the divine, embodying the sun, the wild, and the masculine principle. These archetypal forms provide a framework for understanding the multifaceted nature of the divine and its many expressions in the natural world.

The concept of a dual divinity in Wicca is not exclusive to heterosexual or binary gender perspectives. Wicca is inclusive of diverse gender identities and sexual orientations, and the God and Goddess can be understood and experienced in ways that are relevant to the practitioner. Some Wiccans may work with same-sex God and Goddess pairings or explore non-binary expressions of deity. This flexibility reflects Wicca's commitment to being an inclusive and welcoming spiritual path for all.

Ethical considerations also play an important role in the concept of deity in Wicca. The Wiccan Rede, a central ethical guideline, states, "An it harm none, do what ye will." This principle emphasizes the importance of responsible and ethical behavior and reflects the belief that harming others or the natural world ultimately harms oneself. Wiccans view their ethical obligations as a sacred duty to the God and Goddess and the interconnected web of all life.

In conclusion, the role of deity and the concept of the God and Goddess are fundamental to Wiccan philosophy and spirituality. This dual divinity symbolizes the interplay of masculine and feminine energies in nature and informs every aspect of Wiccan belief and practice. The God and Goddess are viewed as immanent and present in the natural world, allowing for a personal and intimate connection with the divine. Wiccans celebrate the changing attributes of the God and Goddess throughout the Wheel of the Year, perform rituals to invoke their energies, and embrace a fluid and inclusive understanding of deity. Ultimately, in Wicca, the dual divinity serves as a source of inspiration, guidance, and reverence, reminding practitioners of the sacredness of the Earth and their role as stewards of the natural world.

The interconnectedness of all life

The concept of the interconnectedness of all life is a fundamental and cherished belief across a wide range of spiritual traditions and philosophical systems. It underscores the profound idea that every living being, every element of the natural world, and every facet of the universe is intricately linked, forming an intricate web of relationships and dependencies. This concept holds particular significance in indigenous wisdom, ecological philosophies, and spiritual practices such as Buddhism and Wicca. In this section, we will explore the interconnectedness of all life, examining its philosophical foundations, ecological implications, and profound spiritual significance.

At its core, the interconnectedness of all life is a recognition that everything in the universe is interdependent. This interdependence extends to existence's physical, ecological, and spiritual dimensions. It acknowledges that every action has consequences, and that the well-being of one part of the web of life is intimately tied to the well-being of all other parts. This profound insight challenges notions of isolation and separation, emphasizing the unity and coherence of the universe.

In ecological and environmental philosophies, the concept of interconnectedness has profound implications for how humans interact with the natural world. It highlights the idea that human beings are not separate from nature but are an integral part of it. The health and sustainability of ecosystems, from the smallest microorganisms to the largest predators, are intertwined, and disruptions in one part of the web can have far-reaching consequences. This ecological interdependence is a central tenet of sustainability and conservation efforts, emphasizing the importance of preserving biodiversity and safeguarding the delicate balance of ecosystems.

One of the key ecological principles that demonstrates the interconnectedness of all life is the food web concept. In any given ecosystem, organisms are connected through a complex network of predation and competition. Each species' survival and well-being rely on its relationships with others. For example, the decline of a predator species can result in an increase in its prey species, which, in turn, can influence the abundance of plant species that the prey consumes. This ripple effect exemplifies how changes in one part of the web can cascade through the entire ecosystem, illustrating the interconnectedness of all life.

In indigenous wisdom and spiritual traditions, the interconnectedness of all life is often expressed through the concept of animism—the belief that all things possess a spirit or consciousness. Indigenous cultures worldwide have long recognized non-human entities' intrinsic value and agency, from animals and plants to rocks and rivers. This perspective fosters a deep sense of respect and reciprocity with the natural world, as every being is seen as a unique expression of the divine.

Buddhism, a spiritual tradition that strongly emphasizes interconnectedness, teaches the concept of "interbeing." This term, coined by Vietnamese Zen master Thich Nhat Hanh, encapsulates the idea that nothing exists in isolation; everything is connected and dependent on everything else. According to Buddhist teachings, the illusion of a separate self is a source of suffering, and recognizing our interconnected nature is essential for attaining enlightenment and living in harmony with all life.

In Wicca, a contemporary pagan tradition, the interconnectedness of all life is central to its belief in the sacredness of nature. Wiccans view the natural world as a manifestation of divine energy, where every element, plant, and creature possesses inherent value and significance. This reverence for nature is deeply rooted in ancient pagan traditions, where the cycles of the seasons, the phases of the moon, and the changing tides held spiritual significance. Wiccans celebrate and align their rituals with these natural rhythms, recognizing the interconnectedness of all life and the importance of living in harmony with the Earth.

The ethical guidelines in Wicca, such as the Wiccan Rede and the Threefold Law, underscore the interconnectedness of all life. The Wiccan Rede states, "An it harm none, do what ye will," emphasizing the importance of responsible and ethical behavior. It encourages Wiccans to consider the potential consequences of their actions and strive for actions that cause no harm to others or themselves. The Threefold Law, often summarized as "Whatever you send out into the universe, it will return to you threefold," reinforces the idea of karma or cause and effect, suggesting that the consequences of one's actions will come back amplified. This belief serves as a moral compass, guiding Wiccans to act with mindfulness and integrity in all aspects of life, magical or otherwise.

The concept of the interconnectedness of all life is not confined to specific spiritual or ecological perspectives; it has also found resonance in scientific disciplines. Ecology, for instance, studies the complex web of relationships between organisms and their environments. Ecological principles, such as trophic levels and energy flow, demonstrate the interdependence of species and ecosystems. Recognizing ecological interconnections has led to a greater understanding of the importance of biodiversity and the fragile balance of ecosystems.

Quantum physics, at the forefront of modern physics, has also revealed a deep interconnectedness at the subatomic level. Quantum entanglement, a phenomenon where particles become connected in such a way that their properties are interdependent, challenges conventional notions of separateness and locality. It suggests that the boundaries between individual particles are not as distinct as classical physics once thought, pointing to a profound level of interconnectedness in the fabric of reality itself. In

conclusion, the concept of the interconnectedness of all life is a deeply rooted and universal belief that transcends cultural, spiritual, and scientific boundaries. It underscores the interdependence of every living being, the unity of the natural world, and the profound implications for ethical and ecological considerations. Whether expressed through indigenous wisdom, spiritual practices like Buddhism and Wicca, or scientific insights from ecology and quantum physics, the recognition of interconnectedness invites us to see ourselves as an integral part of the intricate web of life, inspiring reverence, responsibility, and a profound sense of unity with all that exists.

The Wheel of the Year and its significance

In the practice of Wicca, a contemporary pagan and nature-based religion, the Wheel of the Year is a sacred and cyclical calendar that marks the changing seasons and the turning points of the natural world. This symbolic wheel consists of eight festivals or Sabbats, spaced evenly throughout the year, each with its unique rituals, symbolism, and significance. The Wheel of the Year is a cornerstone of Wiccan spirituality, guiding practitioners in their connection to the natural world and the cycles of life, death, and rebirth. This section will explore the Wheel of the Year and its profound significance in Wiccan practice and philosophy.

At the heart of the Wheel of the Year is recognizing the cyclical nature of existence. Wiccans view life as an ever-turning wheel, with no beginning or end. This cyclical perspective is deeply rooted in the natural world, where seasons, tides, and celestial events follow predictable patterns, signifying the eternal rhythm of birth, growth, decline, and regeneration. The Wheel embodies this perpetual cycle, inviting practitioners to align themselves with the ebb and flow of nature's energies.

The Wheel of the Year is divided into two main categories of festivals: the Greater Sabbats and the Lesser Sabbats. The Greater Sabbats, also known as the "Fire Festivals," include Samhain, Imbolc, Beltane, and Lammas. These festivals mark the significant turning points of the solar year, such as the solstices and equinoxes. The Lesser Sabbats, also known as the "Earth Festivals," include Yule, Ostara, Litha (or Midsummer), and Mabon. These festivals celebrate the seasons in between the solstices and equinoxes. Each Sabbat has its unique symbolism and themes, reflecting the characteristics of the season it represents.

Samhain, the first of the Greater Sabbats, is celebrated on October 31st and marks the end of the old year and the beginning of the new. It is a time when the veil between the physical and spirit worlds is believed to be thin, making it suitable for honoring ancestors and communing with the deceased. Samhain is a festival of reflection, transformation, and the acceptance of the inevitability of death and rebirth.

Imbolc, celebrated on February 1st or 2nd, heralds the first signs of spring. It is dedicated to the Celtic goddess Brigid and symbolizes the earth's awakening from its winter slumber. Imbolc is a time for purification, inspiration, and recognizing the returning light and life.

Beltane, celebrated on May 1st, marks the height of spring and the beginning of summer. It is a festival of fertility, love, and the sacred marriage of the God and Goddess. Beltane is a time for joyous celebrations, dancing around the Maypole, and embracing the vitality and passion of life.

Lammas, celebrated on August 1st or 2nd, is the first harvest festival of the year. It is a time to give thanks for the abundance of the earth and the fruits of labor. Lammas reminds practitioners of the need for sacrifice, the cyclical nature of the harvest, and the importance of sharing and community.

The Lesser Sabbats, or Earth Festivals, correspond to the equinoxes and solstices. Yule, celebrated on December 21st or 22nd, marks the winter solstice, the year's longest night. It is a festival of light and rebirth, as the days begin to lengthen once again. Yule celebrates the return of the sun and the promise of new beginnings.

Ostara, celebrated on March 21st or 22nd, marks the spring equinox when day and night are in perfect balance. It is a time of renewal, fertility, and the earth's awakening. Ostara celebrates the return of life and the emergence of new growth.

Litha, or Midsummer, celebrated on June 21st or 22nd, marks the summer solstice, the year's longest day. It is a festival of the sun's peak power and the celebration of life's abundance. Litha is a time of illumination, achievement, and the acknowledgment of the sun's life-giving energy.

Mabon, celebrated on September 21st or 22nd, marks the autumnal equinox when day and night are again in balance. It is a harvest and thanksgiving festival, as well as a time of reflection and inner preparation for the coming winter. Mabon highlights the importance of balance and the interconnectedness of all life.

The significance of the Wheel of the Year in Wiccan philosophy is multifaceted. First and foremost, it serves as a spiritual calendar, guiding Wiccans in their rituals, ceremonies, and magical workings. Each Sabbat allows practitioners to attune themselves to the energies of the season, connect with the divine, and reflect on their own spiritual journey.

Moreover, the Wheel of the Year reinforces the concept of interconnectedness. It reminds Wiccans that they are part of a larger cosmic and natural order, where the well-being of one part of the web of life is intimately connected to the well-being of all others. This awareness fosters a sense of responsibility, stewardship, and reverence for the Earth and its cycles.

The Wheel of the Year also encourages mindfulness and living in harmony with the natural world. Wiccans often celebrate the Sabbats outdoors, in natural settings, to immerse themselves in the beauty and energies of the season. This connection with nature serves as a source of inspiration, spiritual growth, and a reminder of the sacredness of the Earth.

In conclusion, the Wheel of the Year is a profound and sacred calendar that is central to Wiccan spirituality and philosophy. Its cyclical nature mirrors the eternal rhythms of life, death, and rebirth found in the natural world. Through its festivals, rituals, and symbolism, the Wheel of the Year deepens the spiritual connection between Wiccans and the Earth, fostering a profound sense of interconnectedness, reverence, and responsibility for all life. It is a powerful reminder of the eternal cycle of existence and the enduring wisdom of nature.

The concept of sacred space in Wiccan practice

In Wicca, a contemporary pagan and nature-based spiritual tradition, the concept of sacred space holds profound significance. It represents an essential element of Wiccan practice, as it serves as the physical and metaphysical setting where rituals, ceremonies, and magical workings take place. Sacred space is more than just a physical location; it is a space that has been consecrated, purified, and imbued with spiritual energy, creating a connection between the practitioner and the divine. This section will explore the concept of sacred space in Wiccan practice, examining its importance, creation, and role in facilitating spiritual experiences.

At the heart of the concept of sacred space in Wicca lies the belief that the physical world reflects the spiritual. Wiccans view all of nature as sacred and believe that the divine can be encountered directly through a personal and intimate connection with the natural world. Therefore, creating a sacred space is a way to manifest and honor this spiritual interconnectedness, transforming an ordinary location into a place where the veil between the mundane and the sacred is thin.

One of the most common methods for creating sacred space in Wiccan practice is through the casting of a ritual circle. The circle represents a boundary that separates the sacred from the profane, the mundane from the spiritual. It acts as a protective barrier that encloses the practitioner and serves as a container for the energies raised during rituals and ceremonies. The casting of the circle involves the visualization of a shimmering sphere of energy, typically created with tools such as an athame (ritual knife) or wand, and often involves reciting specific words or invocations.

The creation of sacred space in Wicca also involves the invocation of the elements—earth, air, fire, water, and spirit. These elements are considered fundamental building blocks of the universe and are revered in their own right. The practitioner calls upon each element to be present and to lend its energies to the sacred space. This elemental invocation not only serves to consecrate the circle but also symbolizes the recognition of the interconnectedness of all life and the alignment with the natural world.

Wiccans often create an altar within the sacred circle—a focal point for rituals and offerings. The altar is typically adorned with symbols, tools, candles, and other items of personal significance. It represents a microcosm of the sacred space and serves as a place for offerings to the divine, as well as a conduit for communication and energy exchange with the spiritual realm.

The cardinal directions—north, east, south, and west—also play a crucial role in the creation of sacred space. Each direction is associated with specific elemental correspondences and symbolic attributes. For example, the east is linked to air and represents the element of intellect and communication, while the south corresponds to fire and symbolizes passion and transformation. By calling upon the directions and their associated energies, Wiccans create a balanced and harmonious sacred space that encompasses the qualities of all four elements.

The concept of sacred space in Wiccan practice extends beyond the physical circle and altar. It also encompasses the practitioner's state of mind and intention. Sacred space is not solely about the external environment but also about the internal shift in consciousness that occurs when one enters the ritual mindset. This shift involves setting aside mundane concerns, opening oneself to the energies of the divine, and embracing a sense of reverence and mindfulness. It is a mental and emotional preparation that allows the practitioner to connect with the spiritual realm and attune to the energies of the ritual or ceremony.

The creation of sacred space is not limited to formal rituals or ceremonies; it can also be applied to everyday magical practices. Many Wiccans incorporate elements of sacred space into their daily routines, such as lighting candles, saying prayers, or performing simple rituals to attune themselves to the divine and set a sacred intention for their day. This practice underscores the belief that every moment and every action can be infused with spiritual significance and connection.

The concept of sacred space in Wicca also plays an essential part in the practice of magic. Within the circle's confines, practitioners work with the energies of the elements, deities, and the natural world to manifest their intentions and desires. The sacred space serves as a container for these energies, allowing them to be concentrated, focused, and directed toward a specific goal. Whether it's divination, healing, or spellcasting, the creation of sacred space provides a structured and powerful framework for magical work.

Furthermore, sacred space in Wicca facilitates communion with the divine. The circle is often seen as a doorway to the spiritual realm, a place where the practitioner can connect with deities, ancestors, and spirit guides. It is a space for receiving guidance, insight, and inspiration from the spiritual realm and for forging a deeper relationship with the divine.

The concept of sacred space in Wicca is closely tied to the idea of reverence for the Earth and the recognition of the interconnectedness of all life. Wiccans believe that by creating and maintaining sacred space, they honor the sacredness of the natural world and their role as stewards of the Earth. This perspective underscores the importance of environmental responsibility and the ethical principles of Wicca, such as the Wiccan Rede, which states, "An it harm none, do what ye will." Sacred space serves as a reminder of the interconnectedness of all life and the sacred duty to act with integrity and respect for the Earth and its creatures.

In conclusion, the concept of sacred space is a foundational and integral aspect of Wiccan practice. It represents the physical and metaphysical setting where rituals, ceremonies, and magical workings occur, bridging the mundane and the sacred. Sacred space involves the casting of a ritual circle, the invocation of the elements, the use of an altar, and the alignment with the cardinal directions. It also encompasses a shift in consciousness and intention, allowing practitioners to connect with the divine, work magic, and honor the interconnectedness of all life. Ultimately, sacred space in Wicca serves as a tangible manifestation of the spiritual connection between the practitioner and the natural world, fostering a profound sense of reverence, responsibility, and spiritual growth.

CHAPTER III

Ethics in Wiccan Practice

The Wiccan Rede: Origins and interpretations

The Wiccan Rede, a central ethical guideline in Wicca, encapsulates the moral and spiritual principles that guide the practice of this contemporary pagan and nature-based religion. Often summarized as "An it harm none, do what ye will," the Rede emphasizes responsible and ethical behavior, underlining the interconnectedness of all life and the consequences of one's actions. In this section, we will explore the origins and interpretations of the Wiccan Rede, delving into its historical development and its role in shaping the ethical framework of Wiccan spirituality.

The Wiccan Rede is a succinct and memorable ethical principle that serves as a moral compass for Wiccans, guiding them in their actions and decisions. The phrase itself, "An it harm none, do what ye will," is often attributed to Doreen Valiente, a prominent figure in the history of modern Wicca and a collaborator with Gerald Gardner, one of the founders of the Wiccan movement. Valiente is credited with crafting this formulation of the Rede, which encapsulates the essence of Wiccan ethics. However, it is essential to recognize that the concept of living in harmony with the natural world and respecting the interconnectedness of all life is an integral part of the broader pagan and folkloric traditions that influenced the development of Wicca.

The origins of the Rede can be traced to earlier folk traditions, where ethical guidelines and aphorisms were passed down through oral tradition. In these traditions, the emphasis on living in harmony with nature, respecting the balance of life, and refraining from causing harm to others was common. These principles found their way into the emerging Wiccan movement in the mid-20th century, as it sought to establish a coherent ethical framework that reflected its reverence for the natural world.

Interpreting the Wiccan Rede involves a nuanced understanding of its language and intent. The phrase "An it harm none, do what ye will" has been subject to various interpretations and discussions within the Wiccan community. One of the key points of contention lies in the definition of harm. What constitutes harm, and how far-reaching are its consequences? Some Wiccans interpret harm narrowly, focusing primarily on physical harm or direct negative impact on others. Others take a broader view, including emotional, psychological, and even spiritual harm within their interpretation.

The phrase "do what ye will" is another aspect that invites diverse interpretations. While it may appear to suggest unrestrained freedom, it is often understood within the context of ethical responsibility. Wiccans interpret this as an injunction to exercise one's will and desires in alignment with the Rede while respecting the well-being of all life. In other words, it encourages personal empowerment and autonomy within a framework of ethical consideration.

A common misconception about the Wiccan Rede is that it advocates moral relativism or a "anything goes" attitude. However, most Wiccans understand that living in harmony with the Rede involves making ethical choices and weighing the potential consequences of their actions. It is not a carte blanche for self-indulgence or disregard for the well-being of others.

Another aspect of the Rede's interpretation concerns the phrase "none." Does "none" refer only to humans, or does it extend to all life, including animals and the environment? Many Wiccans emphasize the interconnectedness of all life and extend the ethical principles of the Rede to encompass the well-being of the natural world. This interpretation aligns with the broader pagan perspective of living in harmony with nature and respecting the sanctity of the Earth.

In practice, the Wiccan Rede informs decision-making and ethical considerations in various aspects of a Wiccan's life. It affects choices related to spellwork, magical workings, daily interactions, and environmental responsibility. For example, when crafting a spell, a Wiccan would consider the ethical implications and potential consequences of the desired outcome. If a spell could potentially harm someone or interfere with their free will, it would go against the principles of the Rede.

Furthermore, the Rede underscores the importance of mindfulness and ethical responsibility in daily life. It encourages Wiccans to consider the impact of their actions on others and the natural world. This perspective aligns with the broader ecological and environmental concerns of many Wiccans, emphasizing the sacred duty to protect and preserve the Earth and its ecosystems. The

Wiccan Rede also intersects with the concept of karma or the Threefold Law, another ethical principle in Wicca. The Threefold Law suggests that the consequences of one's actions will return threefold, amplifying the effects of both positive and negative actions. This belief reinforces the idea that responsible and ethical behavior is not just a matter of moral duty but also an acknowledgment of the interconnectedness of all life and the repercussions of one's choices.

The Wiccan Rede serves as a unifying ethical principle within the diverse and decentralized Wiccan community. While interpretations may vary, the underlying commitment to ethical behavior, environmental responsibility, and the recognition of the interconnectedness of all life remains a common thread among Wiccans. The Rede is not a rigid code but a flexible guideline that invites reflection, personal growth, and ethical consideration in all aspects of life.

In conclusion, the Wiccan Rede, encapsulated in the phrase "An it harm none, do what ye will," represents a core ethical principle in Wicca. Its origins can be traced to earlier folk traditions, and it has evolved to reflect the moral and spiritual principles of modern Wiccan practice. Interpretations of the Rede vary, but its central message emphasizes responsible and ethical behavior, the recognition of harm in all its forms, and the interconnectedness of all life. The Rede serves as a moral compass that informs decision-making, spellwork, and daily interactions, fostering a sense of reverence, responsibility, and mindfulness within the Wiccan community.

The Threefold Law and its implications

The Threefold Law is a fundamental concept within various modern pagan and Wiccan belief systems. It serves as a moral and ethical guideline for practitioners, emphasizing the idea that the energy or intent one puts out into the world will return to them three times as strong. This principle shapes the way individuals conduct themselves in both mundane and magical aspects of their lives, and its implications are far-reaching, impacting not only personal development but also the broader interconnectedness of the universe.

At its core, the Threefold Law revolves around the concept of karma, albeit with a specific focus on the rule of three. In essence, it suggests that whatever energy or intention a person puts forth—be it positive or negative—will come back to them, magnified threefold. This idea fosters a deep sense of responsibility among practitioners, encouraging them to be mindful of their thoughts, words, and actions. It serves as a powerful reminder that the universe operates on a balance of energies, and any disruption can have consequences.

One of the most immediate implications of the Threefold Law is the emphasis on ethical behavior. Practitioners are compelled to act with kindness, compassion, and respect towards others, not only to avoid negative repercussions but also because it aligns with their spiritual values. This ethical framework promotes harmony and goodwill in personal relationships and within the wider community, fostering a sense of interconnectedness that transcends individual boundaries.

Moreover, the Threefold Law encourages introspection and self-improvement. Individuals who follow this belief system understand that their own growth and development are integral to the well-being of the world around them. Consequently, they strive to become better versions of themselves, working on their flaws and negative tendencies. This constant self-reflection and self-improvement contribute to personal growth and enlightenment, allowing practitioners to lead more fulfilling lives.

The Law's implications extend beyond personal development and ethics, touching upon the practice of magic itself. In this context, magic is understood to be the control of energy to achieve desired results. When working with magic, practitioners must be acutely aware of the energy they are harnessing and the intent behind their actions. The Threefold Law cautions that any misuse or manipulation of energy for selfish or harmful purposes will bring about negative consequences. This encourages practitioners to use magic responsibly, for the greater good, and with respect for the natural balance of the universe.

Furthermore, the Threefold Law reinforces the idea of interconnectedness. It emphasizes that all actions have ripple effects, affecting not only the individual but also the broader community and the world at large. This interconnected worldview encourages practitioners to engage in acts of kindness, charity, and environmental stewardship, recognizing that their actions contribute to the overall well-being of the planet. In a time when environmental concerns are paramount, this aspect of the Threefold Law holds particular significance.

Critics may argue that the Threefold Law is merely a superstition or a form of psychological conditioning. They may question the empirical evidence supporting the notion that energy returns threefold. However, from the perspective of those who follow this belief system, it is not necessary to prove the Law's validity empirically. It serves as a symbolic and moral guideline that fosters positive behavior and promotes a sense of responsibility. Whether or not the Law has a metaphysical basis, its impact on individuals and communities is undeniable.

In conclusion, the Threefold Law is a foundational concept within modern pagan and Wiccan belief systems, emphasizing the idea that the energy and intent one puts into the world will come back to them threefold. Its implications are profound, shaping ethical behavior, personal development, magical practices, and a sense of interconnectedness. While it may be subject to criticism from some quarters, its significance to those who follow it lies in its ability to inspire positive actions and encourage individuals to live in harmony with themselves, others, and the universe. The Threefold Law serves as a reminder that our actions have consequences, and in a world deeply in need of balance and harmony, its message remains as relevant as ever.

The concept of free will and personal responsibility

Wicca, a modern pagan and witchcraft tradition, places a strong emphasis on the concepts of free will and personal responsibility. These basic principles are at the core of Wiccan ethics and shape the way practitioners approach their spiritual beliefs and magical practices. In Wicca, the concept of free will underscores the idea that individuals have the autonomy to make choices and decisions, while personal responsibility highlights the accountability for the consequences of those choices. This section explores how these concepts are woven into the fabric of Wicca, guiding Wiccans in their spiritual journeys and magical workings.

In Wicca, the concept of free will is profoundly rooted in the belief that individuals have the inherent right to make their own choices and decisions. This autonomy extends to matters of spirituality and magical practice. Wiccans do not follow a centralized religious authority or dogma, which means that each practitioner has the freedom to develop their own personal relationship with the divine. This autonomy allows Wiccans to choose their own pantheons, deities, and spiritual practices based on their personal beliefs and preferences. While there are common rituals and traditions within Wicca, adherence to them is a matter of personal choice rather than obligation.

The concept of free will in Wicca also extends to the ethical principle known as the Wiccan Rede, which suggests practitioners to "harm none." This principle reflects the belief that individuals should have the freedom to act according to their own will as long as it does not cause harm to others or violate their rights. It encourages practitioners to take into account the consequences of their actions and to make choices that promote harmony and well-being. This ethical guideline reinforces the idea that free will carries with it the responsibility to act ethically and responsibly in all aspects of life.

Personal responsibility is another foundational concept in Wicca. It acknowledges that individuals are accountable for the outcomes of their choices and actions, whether in their mundane lives or within the context of magical practice. Wiccans believe that their thoughts, words, and deeds have a direct impact on the world around them, and they accept responsibility for both the positive and negative consequences of their actions. This sense of accountability extends to their interactions with other beings, their treatment of the environment, and their magical workings.

In magical practice, personal responsibility is closely tied to intention. Wiccans emphasize the importance of setting clear and ethical intentions when working with magic. They recognize that the energy raised and directed in magical rituals can have profound effects, and therefore, practitioners must be mindful of their intentions. This concept aligns with the broader ethical framework of Wicca, ensuring that magical workings are conducted with respect for the principles of harm none and personal responsibility.

Wiccans also believe in the Law of Return, often associated with the Threefold Law, which posits that the energy one puts into the world, whether through magical work or mundane actions, will return to them threefold. This principle reinforces the idea that personal responsibility extends to the consequences of one's actions. Practitioners are encouraged to act in ways that promote positive and harmonious outcomes, recognizing that any harm they cause may return to them with greater intensity.

In Wicca, personal responsibility extends to the ethical use of magical tools and symbols. Practitioners are cautioned against appropriating sacred symbols and/or practices from cultures to which they do not belong, as this can be seen as disrespectful and culturally insensitive. Wiccans emphasize the importance of respecting the cultural origins and traditions of magical tools and practices, reinforcing the concept of personal responsibility in the context of cultural sensitivity.

Wiccans also recognize the importance of consent in magical practice. Just as personal responsibility requires practitioners to act ethically and responsibly, it also demands that they seek the consent of others when involving them in magical workings. This is particularly relevant when performing rituals on behalf of others, as respecting their autonomy and consent is considered essential.

The relationship between free will and personal responsibility in Wicca is further underscored by the idea of initiation and dedication. Wiccans often undergo a period of study, self-discovery, and spiritual growth before choosing to be initiated into a coven or dedicating themselves to the craft. This process reflects the autonomy of the individual, who freely chooses to commit to the Wiccan path and accept the responsibilities and ethical principles associated with it.

In conclusion, the concepts of free will and personal responsibility are integral to Wicca, guiding practitioners in their spiritual journeys and magical practices. Wiccans believe in the inherent right of individuals to make their own choices and decisions, both in matters of spirituality and magical workings. At the same time, they emphasize the importance of personal responsibility, encouraging practitioners to act ethically, consider the consequences of their actions, and uphold the principles of harm none. These concepts form the ethical foundation of Wicca, shaping the way practitioners engage with their beliefs and interact with the world around them.

Ethical considerations in magical work

The practice of magic, whether in the realms of witchcraft, Wicca, or other mystical traditions, often involves the manipulation of energy, the invocation of spiritual forces, and the pursuit of desired outcomes. While these practices can be deeply spiritual and transformative, they also raise important ethical considerations. Practitioners of magic must grapple with questions related to intention, responsibility, and the consequences of their actions. This section explores the ethical dimensions of magical work, examining how ethical principles shape magical practice and influence the outcomes of such endeavors.

One of the fundamental ethical principles in magical work is the notion that practitioners should strive to harm none. This principle, often associated with Wiccan and pagan traditions, is known as the Wiccan Rede. It encourages practitioners to be mindful of the potential consequences of their magical actions and to avoid using their powers to cause harm or suffering to others. This ethical guideline reflects a commitment to moral responsibility and emphasizes the interconnectedness of all living beings.

Intention is another crucial aspect of ethical magical practice. Practitioners are encouraged to examine their motivations and intentions behind their magical workings. This introspective process helps individuals align their magical pursuits with their ethical values. It also emphasizes the importance of being clear and specific about one's intentions, as the energy raised and directed in magical rituals can have unintended consequences if not properly focused.

The concept of consent is paramount in ethical magical work. Just as it is unethical to harm others through magical means without their consent, it is also important to seek permission when involving others in magical workings. This is particularly relevant when performing healing or protection spells on behalf of others, as respecting their autonomy and consent is essential.

Ethical considerations extend to the use of magical tools and symbols. Practitioners must be cautious about appropriating sacred symbols or practices from cultures they do not belong to, as this can be seen as disrespectful and culturally insensitive. It is vital to approach other cultures with reverence and a willingness to learn, rather than appropriating their practices for personal gain.

The ethical use of divination is another aspect of magical practice that requires careful consideration. Divination tools, including tarot cards or pendulums, can provide valuable insights and guidance. However, practitioners must use these tools responsibly and avoid using them to invade others' privacy or manipulate outcomes to their advantage.

A significant ethical dilemma arises when practitioners engage in magic for personal gain or to influence the will of others. Love spells and money spells, for example, raise questions about consent and ethical boundaries. Some argue that such practices infringe upon the free will of others and can lead to negative consequences. Ethical magical practitioners often stress the importance of focusing on self-improvement and personal growth rather than attempting to manipulate external circumstances or individuals.

The Law of Return, often associated with the Threefold Law, is a central ethical concept in many magical traditions. It posits that the energy one puts into the world, whether through magical work or mundane actions, will return to them threefold. This principle reinforces the idea that ethical behavior and responsible magical practice are essential for one's own well-being. It serves as a reminder that one cannot escape the consequences of their actions, and that any harm caused to others may ultimately harm oneself.

Another consideration in magical ethics is the responsibility to clean up any magical messes or unintended consequences. If a magical working does not yield the desired outcome or has unforeseen negative effects, practitioners are encouraged to take responsibility for rectifying the situation. This may involve performing rituals to undo or mitigate the effects of a previous working, as well as learning from the experience to avoid similar mistakes in the future.

The concept of secrecy and discretion is also important in ethical magical practice. While some practitioners choose to openly discuss their magical work, others prefer to keep their practices private. Respecting the confidentiality and privacy of others' magical workings is a matter of ethical consideration, as is the responsibility to protect the identities and personal information of individuals involved in any magical activities.

In conclusion, ethical considerations are a crucial part of magical work. Practitioners must navigate complex moral questions related to intention, consent, responsibility, and the consequences of their actions. Ethical magical practice is not only about achieving desired outcomes but also about cultivating a sense of moral responsibility, respect for others, and an awareness of the interconnectedness of all living beings. By adhering to ethical principles, magical practitioners can create a more harmonious and spiritually fulfilling practice that aligns with their values and beliefs.

The role of divination in ethical decision-making

Divination is a practice that holds a significant place within Wicca, a modern pagan and witchcraft tradition. It serves as a means of seeking guidance, insights, and answers from the divine or spiritual realms. In the context of ethical decision-making, divination plays a crucial role for Wiccans. It helps practitioners navigate complex choices, align their actions with their values, and ensure that they are acting in harmony with the principles of harm none and personal responsibility that are central to Wiccan ethics. This section explores the multifaceted role of divination in ethical decision-making within the Wiccan tradition.

One of the primary functions of divination in Wicca is to provide clarity and insight into difficult decisions. When faced with complex moral dilemmas or choices that could have far-reaching consequences, Wiccans often turn to divination as a tool for seeking guidance. Divination methods, such as tarot card readings, pendulum dowsing, or scrying, allow practitioners to tap into their intuition and interact with the spiritual energies to gain a deeper understanding of the situation at hand. This process helps Wiccans make more informed decisions by shedding light on potential outcomes and highlighting aspects of the situation that may not be immediately apparent.

In ethical decision-making, divination serves as a means of seeking alignment with one's higher self and ethical principles. Wiccans believe that divination can help them discern the ethical implications of their choices and whether a particular course of action is in harmony with their spiritual values. By consulting divination tools, they can evaluate the potential consequences of their decisions from a moral perspective. This allows practitioners to act in accordance with their principles of harm none and personal responsibility, ensuring that their choices are ethically sound.

Furthermore, divination can aid Wiccans in identifying any hidden or unconscious biases that may influence their decision-making. When confronted with ethical dilemmas, individuals may be unaware of underlying prejudices or preconceived notions that cloud their judgment. Divination provides a means of accessing intuitive insights that go beyond conscious thought, allowing practitioners to uncover any biases or blind spots that may affect their ethical choices. This self-awareness is essential for making ethical decisions that are free from personal biases and rooted in objective consideration.

Another important aspect of divination in ethical decision-making is its role in exploring alternative perspectives and outcomes. Ethical dilemmas often involve competing values and interests, making it challenging to determine the most morally sound course of action. Divination can help practitioners consider different scenarios and potential consequences, enabling them to weigh the ethical implications of each option. This process encourages a more holistic approach to decision-making, one that takes into account the broader ethical context and the interconnectedness of all living beings.

In Wicca, divination also serves as a tool for connecting with spiritual guides, deities, or higher powers that can offer guidance and wisdom in ethical decision-making. Many Wiccans believe that divination rituals create a sacred space in which they can commune with their chosen deities or spirit guides. Through divination, practitioners can seek the counsel and blessings of these spiritual entities, asking for their insights and guidance in navigating moral choices. This connection with the divine reinforces the sense of responsibility and accountability that Wiccans feel toward their ethical decisions.

Moreover, divination can be instrumental in addressing questions related to personal growth and spiritual development. Ethical decision-making in Wicca is not only about choosing the right course of action but also about individual growth and self-improvement. Divination can provide practitioners with insights into their own spiritual journeys, helping them understand how their choices align with their personal path and spiritual goals. This self-reflection encourages a deeper commitment to ethical living and personal responsibility.

It is important to note that divination in Wicca is not seen as a deterministic or fortune-telling practice. Instead, it is considered a tool for gaining insights and guidance, offering possibilities rather than definitive answers. Wiccans understand that they still have the freedom to make choices based on the information obtained through divination. Divination is a means of empowerment, enabling practitioners to make informed and ethical decisions while acknowledging their free will and autonomy.

In conclusion, divination plays a multifaceted role in ethical decision-making within the Wiccan tradition. It serves as a source of guidance, clarity, and insight when faced with complex moral dilemmas. Divination helps practitioners align their choices with their values and principles, identify unconscious biases, consider alternative perspectives, and connect with higher powers for counsel. Moreover, it encourages personal growth and self-improvement, reinforcing the commitment to ethical living and personal responsibility. In Wicca, divination is not a passive or deterministic practice but a tool that empowers individuals to make ethical decisions that are in harmony with their spiritual beliefs and principles.

CHAPTER IV

Ethical Enchantments: Spellwork and Ritual

How spells and rituals are used in Wiccan practice

Wicca, a modern pagan and witchcraft tradition, is characterized by its rich tapestry of rituals and spells. These magical practices serve as a means of connecting with the divine, harnessing natural energies, and manifesting desired outcomes. Spells and rituals are integral to Wiccan spirituality, offering practitioners a structured and meaningful way to engage with their beliefs and the forces of nature. This section explores the role of spells and rituals in Wiccan practice, highlighting their significance, components, and the purposes they serve.

Spells and rituals in Wicca are a means of focusing intention and energy to achieve specific goals or outcomes. They are considered a way of working in harmony with the natural world, the cycles of the moon, and the energies of the elements. Wiccans believe that by performing these rituals and spells, they can tap into the spiritual and metaphysical forces that surround them, allowing them to effectuate positive changes in their lives and the world around them.

Central to Wiccan rituals and spells is the concept of sacred space. Practitioners typically begin by creating a sacred circle, which serves as a boundary between the mundane world and the spiritual realm. This circle is often cast using tools like a wand or an athame, and it is believed to contain and amplify the energy raised during the ritual. The circle represents the interconnectedness of all living beings and the protection it provides from negative energies.

The casting of a circle is followed by the invocation of the four elements: Earth, Air, Fire, and Water. Each element is associated with certain qualities and energies, and they are called upon to lend their strength and support to the ritual. For example, Earth represents stability and grounding, while Air signifies intellect and communication. By invoking these elements, Wiccans aim to balance and harmonize their energies within the sacred space.

Deity invocation is another essential component of Wiccan rituals and spells. Wiccans may call upon specific gods and goddesses, often from various pantheons, depending on the nature of the working. These deities are seen as manifestations of the divine, representing different aspects of existence and the natural world. The deities are invited to witness and engage in the ritual, and their energies are invoked to aid in achieving the desired outcomes.

The phases of the moon hold great significance in Wiccan practice, and many rituals and spells are performed in alignment with lunar cycles. The New Moon is often associated with new beginnings and intentions, while the Full Moon is considered a time of culmination and manifestation. Wiccans believe that the moon's energy can enhance the potency of their magical workings, and they time their rituals accordingly.

Candles, herbs, crystals, and other magical tools are commonly used in Wiccan spells and rituals to amplify intention and energy. The choice of colors, scents, and correspondences of these tools is carefully considered, as each element is believed to have its own unique vibrational energy that can be harnessed to strengthen the magical working. For example, a green candle may be used in a spell for prosperity, while rose quartz crystals may be employed in a love spell.

Visualization and meditation are crucial aspects of Wiccan magical practice. During rituals and spells, practitioners often engage in deep meditation and visualization to connect with their inner selves and the energies they are working with. They focus their thoughts and intentions on the desired outcome, using the power of their minds to direct energy toward their goals. This mental concentration and visualization are essential components of effective spellcasting.

One of the key principles in Wicca is the concept of the "Threefold Law" or the "Law of Return." This principle posits that the energy one puts into the world, whether through magical work or mundane actions, will return to them threefold. Therefore, ethical considerations are significant in Wiccan spellcasting and ritual work. Practitioners are encouraged to use their magical powers responsibly and in alignment with the ethical principles of harm none and personal responsibility.

In Wiccan practice, spells and rituals serve a wide range of purposes. They can be used for healing, protection, divination, empowerment, love, fertility, prosperity, and more. Some rituals are dedicated to celebrating the cycles of nature, such as the Sabbats, which mark the solstices, equinoxes, and other significant points in the annual calendar. Others may be dedicated to rites of passage, such as handfastings (Wiccan weddings) or initiations into covens.

Moreover, Wiccan rituals and spells are not limited to solitary practice. Many Wiccans choose to work in covens, which are organized groups of practitioners who come together to perform rituals, share knowledge, and support each other on their spiritual journeys. Coven rituals often involve the collaboration of multiple practitioners, each contributing their energy and intentions to the working.

In conclusion, spells and rituals are a central and vibrant aspect of Wiccan practice. They offer a structured and meaningful way for practitioners to engage with their spiritual beliefs, connect with the divine, and harness natural energies to manifest their intentions. These rituals and spells involve the creation of sacred space, invocation of elements and deities, alignment with lunar cycles, and the use of magical tools, visualization, and meditation. Ethical considerations are also paramount in Wiccan spellcasting, emphasizing the importance of using magical powers responsibly and in accordance with the principles of harm none and personal responsibility. Ultimately, Wiccan rituals and spells serve as a powerful means of transformation, empowerment, and spiritual connection for those who practice this ancient and evolving tradition.

Crafting ethical spells and rituals

In the realm of magic and the occult, ethical considerations play a crucial role in spellcasting and ritual work. Crafting ethical spells and rituals is not just a matter of personal preference; it is an essential aspect of responsible and spiritually meaningful practice. Ethical considerations guide practitioners in ensuring that their magical workings are aligned with principles of harm none, personal responsibility, and respect for the interconnectedness of all living beings. This section explores the importance of ethics in magical practice, offering insights into how ethical spells and rituals are crafted and the impact they have on both practitioners and the world around them.

At the heart of ethical spellcraft and ritual work is the principle of "harm none." This ethical guideline underscores the idea that magical practitioners should avoid causing harm or suffering to others through their magical actions. Whether intentionally or unintentionally, spells and rituals have the potential to influence the lives and well-being of individuals and the world at large. Therefore, practitioners bear a responsibility to consider the potential consequences of their magical workings and to act in ways that promote harmony, well-being, and respect for all living beings.

Intention is a critical factor in crafting ethical spells and rituals. Practitioners must be clear about their intentions and motivations when engaging in magical work. This clarity of intention ensures that the energy raised and directed during the spell or ritual is aligned with the practitioner's ethical values and objectives. Ethical practitioners take time to reflect on their goals, ensuring that they are in harmony with the principle of harm none and do not infringe upon the free will or well-being of others.

In ethical spellcraft, practitioners often utilize the concept of consent. Just as consent is essential in interpersonal relationships, it is also relevant in magical practice. When performing spells or rituals that involve other individuals, such as healing or protection work, practitioners should seek the consent of those individuals. Respecting the autonomy and boundaries of others is a fundamental ethical principle, and it applies to magical workings as well. Consent ensures that individuals are willing participants in the magical process and that their free will is honored.

Additionally, ethical spellcraft often involves considering the broader implications of one's actions. Practitioners recognize that their magical workings are part of a larger web of existence, affecting not only individuals but also the environment, the community, and the interconnectedness of all living beings. Ethical practitioners take into account how their magical actions may ripple outward, considering the potential consequences on a larger scale. This awareness fosters a sense of responsibility and an understanding of the interconnected nature of all things.

The choice of magical tools, symbols, and correspondences is another aspect of crafting ethical spells and rituals. Practitioners must be mindful of the cultural and spiritual significance of these elements and avoid appropriating sacred symbols or practices from cultures to which they do not belong. Ethical practitioners approach other cultures with respect, reverence, and a willingness to learn, rather than using their practices for personal gain. This cultural sensitivity is a reflection of the ethical principle of respecting the beliefs and practices of others.

The timing of magical workings also plays a role in ethical spellcraft. Many practitioners align their rituals and spells with natural cycles, including the phases of the moon or the seasons. This timing is chosen to harmonize with the energies of the natural world, enhancing the effectiveness of the magical working. Ethical spellcasters consider the timing of their rituals carefully, ensuring that their actions are in sync with the rhythms of nature and the spiritual significance of the chosen timing.

Furthermore, the ethical use of divination is an integral aspect of crafting ethical spells and rituals. Divination tools, such as pendulums, tarot cards, or scrying mirrors, are used to gain insights and guidance from the divine or spiritual realms. Ethical practitioners use divination responsibly, avoiding invasive or manipulative questions that violate the privacy or free will of others. They also respect the boundaries of divination by not using it as a means to predict the future with absolute certainty but as a tool for gaining insights and guidance.

Ethical practitioners understand that magic is not a guarantee of desired outcomes. While spells and rituals can focus intention and energy toward a specific goal, the outcome may still be influenced by a multitude of factors, including free will, external circumstances, and the natural flow of events. Ethical spellcraft acknowledges the limitations of magic and accepts that not all desires can or should be fulfilled through magical means.

In conclusion, crafting ethical spells and rituals is an integral aspect of responsible magical practice. It ensures that practitioners align their magical work with principles of harm none, personal responsibility, and respect for the interconnectedness of all living beings. Ethical spellcraft involves clear intentions, consent, cultural sensitivity, consideration of broader consequences, and alignment with natural cycles. It recognizes that magic is a tool for personal and spiritual growth, transformation, and empowerment, and that its ethical use fosters a sense of responsibility toward the well-being of all living beings and the world we share. Ultimately, ethical spells and rituals are a reflection of the ethical values and principles that guide practitioners on their magical journeys.

Examples of ethical enchantments, including healing, protection, and empowerment spells

Enchantments, a form of magical practice, have been utilized by various cultures throughout history for various purposes. Within the world of enchantments, ethical considerations play a critical role in ensuring that these magical workings align with principles of harm none, personal responsibility, and respect for the interconnectedness of all living beings. In this section, we will explore examples of ethical enchantments, with a focus on healing, protection, and empowerment spells. These enchantments serve as tools for personal and spiritual growth, as well as for the betterment of the world and those who inhabit it.

Healing spells are among the most commonly practiced and ethically sound enchantments. They are crafted with the intention of promoting physical, emotional, or spiritual healing for oneself or others. Healing enchantments often involve the use of herbs, crystals, candles, or other magical tools, as well as the power of visualization and intention. For instance, a practitioner may craft a healing spell to alleviate physical pain or illness, soothe emotional wounds, or aid in the recovery of a loved one. Ethical considerations in healing spells emphasize the importance of respecting an individual's free will and consent, as well as ensuring that the healing process is aligned with the person's highest good.

Protection spells are another category of ethical enchantments designed to shield individuals, spaces, or objects from harm. These spells serve as a means of creating a protective barrier against unfavorable energies, psychic attacks, or physical threats. Protection enchantments can involve the use of amulets, charms, sigils, or incantations, and they often call upon the assistance of deities or spiritual guides associated with protection. Ethical considerations in protection spells emphasize the importance of using defensive magic solely for self-defense or the defense of others when necessary, rather than as a means of aggression or harm. Practitioners of protection magic aim to create a safe and secure environment without infringing on the free will or well-being of others.

Empowerment spells are crafted with the intention of enhancing an individual's self-confidence, inner strength, and personal growth. These enchantments focus on harnessing one's potential and tapping into their inner resources to overcome challenges and obstacles. Empowerment spells often involve affirmations, meditation, visualization, or the use of symbolic items such as talismans or crystals. The ethical considerations in empowerment spells revolve around the principle of encouraging personal growth and self-empowerment without seeking to control or manipulate others. Practitioners aim to inspire confidence, resilience, and a sense of personal agency in themselves or those for whom the spell is cast.

In the realm of healing enchantments, an example of an ethical spell might be a self-healing ritual. A practitioner could create a sacred space, cast a protective circle, and call upon healing energies or deities associated with health and well-being. Through visualization and meditation, they may focus on their own physical or emotional ailments, directing healing energy toward the areas in need. The intention of the spell is to promote their own well-being and recovery, aligning with the ethical principle of self-care and personal responsibility.

A protection spell example is the creation of a protective amulet or charm. The practitioner might craft a talisman using specific herbs, crystals, or symbols associated with protection, while imbuing it with their intention for safety and security. This enchanted item can be carried or worn as a protective shield against unfavorable energies or harmful influences. The ethical aspect of this spell involves using protective magic for the purpose of safeguarding oneself or others without infringing upon the free will or well-being of others.

An empowerment spell could involve a self-confidence and self-love ritual. The practitioner might create a personal affirmation or mantra that promotes self-esteem and self-worth. They would then repeat this affirmation regularly, either during meditation or as part of their daily routine, to cultivate a sense of empowerment and self-belief. This ethical enchantment focuses on personal growth and self-empowerment, encouraging the practitioner to recognize their own inner strength and potential without seeking to control or manipulate others.

In all these examples of ethical enchantments, the practitioner's intention, consent, and ethical responsibility are of paramount importance. They align their magical workings with the principles of harm none and personal responsibility, ensuring that their actions are in harmony with their values and beliefs. These enchantments serve as tools for personal and spiritual growth, promoting well-being, protection, and empowerment without infringing on the free will or well-being of others.

In conclusion, ethical enchantments, including healing, protection, and empowerment spells, are integral to responsible magical practice. They allow practitioners to tap into the transformative power of magic while upholding ethical principles that promote harm none, personal responsibility, and respect for the interconnectedness of all living beings. These enchantments serve as tools for enhancing one's well-being, creating protective barriers, and fostering personal growth, all while honoring the ethical guidelines that guide magical practice. By crafting and casting ethical enchantments, practitioners harness the positive forces of magic to create a better and more harmonious world for themselves and those around them.

The importance of intention in spellwork

In the world of magic and the occult, intention stands as a fundamental and powerful force that underpins spellwork. Whether casting spells for healing, protection, love, or any other purpose, the practitioner's intention is a key element that shapes the outcome of their magical working. Intentions are the driving force behind the energy raised and directed during a spell, and they play an important role in determining the effectiveness and ethical nature of the magical practice. In this section, we will delve into the significance of intention in spellwork, exploring how it influences the magical process, aligns with ethical principles, and empowers practitioners on their spiritual journey.

At its core, intention in spellwork refers to the specific purpose or goal a practitioner seeks to achieve through their magical working. It is the clarity of intention that guides the practitioner's thoughts, emotions, and energy toward the desired outcome. An intention serves as the foundation upon which the entire spell is built, providing focus and direction to the magical energies being harnessed. The act of setting an intention is, in itself, a deliberate and conscious act that initiates the spellwork.

One of the essential aspects of intention in spellwork is its role in shaping the energy raised and directed during the magical working. Practitioners often engage in various rituals, incantations, and visualizations to concentrate their intention and energy on the desired outcome. The intention acts as a beacon that attracts and channels the energies of the universe, focusing them on the specific goal of the spell. For instance, in a healing spell, the practitioner's intention to promote physical or emotional healing directs the energy toward that purpose, amplifying the effectiveness of the working.

The relationship between intention and the ethical nature of spellwork is profound. Ethical considerations, such as the principle of harm none, personal responsibility, and respect for free will, are inherently tied to the intention behind a spell. Ethical spellcraft emphasizes that intentions should be aligned with positive and constructive goals, avoiding any harm or manipulation of others. Practitioners who uphold ethical principles take great care to ensure that their intentions are in harmony with these values. They strive to use their magical powers responsibly and for the betterment of themselves and the world.

Consent is an important ethical consideration directly related to intention in spellwork. When performing spells that involve others, such as love or healing spells, practitioners must seek the consent of the individuals involved. Respecting their autonomy and free will is paramount, and the intention behind the spell should align with the well-being and desires of all parties. This ethical approach ensures that the intention of the spell respects the rights and boundaries of others, promoting harmonious relationships and ethical magical practice.

Another crucial aspect of intention in spellwork is the ethical principle of personal responsibility. Practitioners acknowledge that they are accountable for the consequences of their actions and intentions. Therefore, setting a clear and ethical intention is an act of personal responsibility. It involves considering the potential impact of the spell on oneself and others and ensuring that the intention is aligned with the practitioner's values and beliefs. Personal responsibility extends to all aspects of spellwork, from the initial intention to the execution of the ritual and the acceptance of the outcomes.

Intention in spellwork also plays a significant role in the Law of Attraction, a universal principle that suggests that like attracts like. According to this principle, the intention set during a spell sends out a vibrational energy that resonates with similar energies in the universe. Therefore, a positive and well-defined intention is more likely to attract positive and desired outcomes. For example, a practitioner seeking love will set an intention for a loving and healthy relationship, thereby aligning their energy with those qualities and increasing the likelihood of attracting such a relationship into their life.

Furthermore, the clarity of intention enhances the practitioner's focus and determination in spellwork. A well-defined intention serves as a constant reminder of the goal and purpose of the spell, helping the practitioner stay committed and concentrated throughout the ritual. It also aids in visualization, as the practitioner can more vividly imagine the desired outcome when the intention is clear. This heightened focus contributes to the effectiveness of the spell, as it channels the practitioner's energy and consciousness toward the intention.

Intentions in spellwork are not limited to personal goals and desires; they can also serve broader and altruistic purposes. Some practitioners use their magical abilities to set intentions for the betterment of the world, such as environmental healing, peace, or social justice. In these cases, the intention becomes a force for positive change on a larger scale. Ethical intentions that seek to benefit not only the practitioner but also the greater good reflect a profound understanding of the interconnectedness of all living beings and the responsibility to contribute to a harmonious world.

In conclusion, intention is a fundamental and transformative element in spellwork. It guides the practitioner's thoughts, emotions, and energy toward a specific goal and shapes the magical working from beginning to end. The clarity of intention enhances focus, channels energy, and aligns with ethical principles, such as harm none, personal responsibility, and respect for free will. Setting an ethical intention is an act of conscious and deliberate magic that empowers the practitioner to effect positive change in their life and the world around them. By understanding the profound significance of intention in spellwork, practitioners can deepen their connection to the magical arts and embrace a responsible and ethical approach to their practice.

Ethics of working with deities and spirits in rituals

In the realm of spirituality and magical practice, working with deities and spirits holds a significant place. Many belief systems and traditions involve rituals and ceremonies in which practitioners seek to connect with divine beings, ancestors, or otherworldly entities. These interactions can be profoundly transformative, providing guidance, empowerment, and spiritual growth. However, the ethics of working with deities and spirits in rituals are complex and multifaceted. Practitioners must navigate issues related to consent, respect, cultural sensitivity, and personal responsibility to ensure that their engagements with these beings are ethical and meaningful. In this section, we will explore the ethical considerations that arise when working with deities and spirits in rituals, shedding light on the principles that guide practitioners in their spiritual interactions.

One of the central ethical considerations in working with deities and spirits is the issue of consent. Consent implies that these beings, whether divine or ancestral, have the autonomy to choose whether they wish to engage with practitioners. In many belief systems, deities and spirits are regarded as entities with their own will and agency. Therefore, practitioners must be cautious about assuming that these beings are always willing to participate in rituals or to answer their requests. Ethical practitioners seek consent by invoking or inviting these entities respectfully, while also being prepared to accept if the invitation is declined or if the response is unclear.

Respect is another cornerstone of ethical engagement with deities and spirits. Practitioners approach these beings with reverence and humility, acknowledging their wisdom, power, and potential to influence their lives. This respect extends to the cultural and historical contexts in which these beings are revered. Many deities and spirits are deeply rooted in specific cultural traditions, and ethical practitioners avoid appropriating or misrepresenting these traditions. Instead, they take the time to study and understand the cultural context of the beings they work with, showing respect for the beliefs and practices of the communities that venerate them.

Cultural sensitivity is closely related to respect when working with deities and spirits. Ethical practitioners avoid cultural appropriation, which involves borrowing or imitating elements of another culture without understanding or respecting their significance. Instead, they engage in cross-cultural exploration with a willingness to learn and show respect for the cultural origins of the beings they work with. Practitioners recognize that their spiritual practices should not harm or disrespect the cultures from which these deities and spirits originate.

Personal responsibility is a key ethical principle that guides practitioners in their interactions with deities and spirits. It underscores the idea that individuals are accountable for their actions and their intentions in magical and ritual work. When working with these beings, practitioners must be mindful of the consequences of their requests or offerings. They should consider the potential impact on their own lives, as well as on the wider community, environment, or the beings themselves. Practitioners embrace personal responsibility by carefully considering the ethical implications of their rituals and ensuring that their intentions are aligned with harm none and positive outcomes.

Moreover, reciprocity is an important aspect of ethical interactions with deities and spirits. Many traditions emphasize the concept of giving in return for receiving, whether it's through offerings, gratitude, or service. Ethical practitioners recognize that these beings are not obligated to grant their requests and that building a reciprocal relationship involves giving as well as receiving. They offer gifts, express gratitude, or engage in acts of service to maintain a harmonious and mutually beneficial connection with these entities.

Transparency is a guiding ethical principle in working with deities and spirits. Practitioners should be clear and honest in their communications with these beings, as well as with themselves and their community. This transparency extends to the disclosure of the cultural origins of the beings they work with and the recognition of any cultural boundaries or restrictions associated with them. Practitioners avoid misrepresenting their interactions or experiences, promoting honesty and authenticity in their spiritual practice.

Ethical practitioners also consider the potential consequences of their rituals on their own well-being and mental health. Engaging with deities and spirits can be deeply transformative and intense. Therefore, it is essential to maintain personal boundaries, practice self-care, and seek support or guidance from experienced mentors or spiritual leaders when necessary. Ethical practitioners prioritize their own mental and emotional health to ensure that their interactions with these beings are beneficial and sustainable.

Furthermore, practitioners should be cautious about making grandiose claims or seeking undue influence or power through their interactions with deities and spirits. Ethical engagements with these beings are not about acquiring special privileges or manipulating the supernatural for personal gain. Instead, they focus on spiritual growth, guidance, and personal development while respecting the boundaries and autonomy of the beings involved.

In conclusion, the ethics of working with deities and spirits in rituals are multifaceted and require practitioners to navigate complex considerations. Consent, respect, cultural sensitivity, personal responsibility, reciprocity, transparency, and self-care are all vital principles that guide ethical engagement with these beings. By embracing these principles, practitioners ensure that their interactions are meaningful, respectful, and aligned with the principles of harm none and personal growth. Working with deities and spirits can be a transformative and empowering aspect of spiritual practice, provided that it is approached with mindfulness, integrity, and ethical responsibility.

CHAPTER V

Nurturing the Soul

Meditation and mindfulness in Wiccan practice

Meditation and mindfulness are integral components of Wiccan practice, a modern pagan and witchcraft tradition rooted in the reverence of nature and the worship of various deities. These contemplative practices are crucial in deepening one's spiritual connection, enhancing magical abilities, and fostering personal growth. Within the framework of Wicca, meditation and mindfulness serve as tools for grounding, centering, and connecting with the divine energies of the natural world. This section will explore the importance of meditation and mindfulness in Wiccan practice, how they are incorporated into rituals and daily life, and the transformative power they offer to practitioners.

Meditation in Wiccan practice often involves entering into a state of deep concentration, visualization, or relaxation to facilitate communion with deities, spirits, or the energies of nature. It is a means of quieting the mind and focusing the practitioner's consciousness on a specific intention or purpose. Many Wiccans utilize meditation as a foundational practice to attune themselves to the natural world, harness their magical abilities, and gain insight into their spiritual path.

One common form of meditation in Wicca is guided visualization. During guided visualization, practitioners enter a meditative state and are led through a mental journey by a facilitator or their own imagination. This journey often involves visiting sacred spaces, encountering deities or spirit guides, and experiencing symbolic or meaningful encounters. Guided visualizations are employed to deepen one's connection with the divine and to gain insights, healing, or guidance from the spiritual realm.

Mindfulness, on the other hand, is a practice rooted in present-moment awareness. It involves being fully attentive to one's thoughts, feelings, bodily sensations, and the environment without any judgment or distraction. Mindfulness is often integrated into daily life and ritual in Wicca to foster a heightened sense of awareness and appreciation for the natural world. Practitioners use mindfulness to deepen their connection to the elements, the cycles of nature, and the energies of the earth.

One of the central ways in which meditation and mindfulness are incorporated into Wiccan practice is through the casting and closing of the sacred circle. The casting of the circle is a ritual act in which practitioners create a consecrated and protected space in which magical work can take place. During this process, individuals may engage in focused meditation to ground themselves, center their energies, and attune to the elements. This meditation is essential for creating a sacred and energetically charged environment in which rituals can be performed.

Similarly, mindfulness is emphasized in the elemental invocations and quarter calls that are common in Wiccan rituals. These invocations, which call upon the energies of the four elements (Earth, Air, Fire, and Water), often include contemplative elements that encourage practitioners to connect with the qualities and energies associated with each element. For instance, when invoking the element of Water, practitioners may be encouraged to reflect on the fluidity and emotions within themselves, fostering a sense of emotional awareness and connection to the element.

The Wheel of the Year, which is a series of eight seasonal festivals celebrated in Wicca, also incorporates mindfulness into the practice. Each of these festivals, such as Samhain, Beltane, and Litha, marks a specific point in the natural cycle and celebrates the changing of the seasons. Practitioners engage in mindfulness by observing the natural world, taking time to appreciate the unique energies and qualities of each season. For example, during the festival of Imbolc, which marks the first signs of spring, Wiccans may practice mindfulness by observing the budding of trees, the lengthening of daylight, and the awakening of the earth.

Additionally, meditation and mindfulness play a central role in spellwork and divination within Wicca. Before performing a spell or engaging in divinatory practices, practitioners often enter a meditative state to clear their minds, focus their intentions, and align their energies with the magical goal. This meditative preparation enhances the effectiveness of the magical working and ensures that the practitioner's energy is attuned to their intention.

Furthermore, mindfulness is employed in divination practices such as scrying, tarot card readings, and pendulum dowsing. Practitioners approach these forms of divination with a clear and open mind, fully present in the moment, and attuned to their inner guidance. By cultivating mindfulness, individuals can sharpen their intuitive abilities and gain deeper insights into their spiritual path and life circumstances.

In Wiccan practice, meditation and mindfulness are seen as transformative tools that offer numerous benefits to practitioners. They provide a means of attuning to the natural world, fostering a profound connection with the elements and the cycles of nature. These practices also enhance one's magical abilities by honing concentration, visualization, and energy manipulation skills. Additionally, meditation and mindfulness promote self-awareness and personal growth by promoting individuals to explore their inner landscapes, emotions, and spiritual insights.

In conclusion, meditation and mindfulness are integral aspects of Wiccan practice, serving as tools for grounding, centering, and connecting with the divine energies of the natural world. These contemplative practices are woven into rituals, daily life, and magical workings, fostering a deeper connection to the elements, the cycles of nature, and the energies of the earth. By incorporating meditation and mindfulness into their practice, Wiccans enhance their spiritual journey, deepen their magical abilities, and cultivate a profound sense of awareness and reverence for the natural world.

Different meditation techniques in Wicca

Meditation is a central practice in many spiritual and mystical traditions, and Wicca is no exception. Wicca, a contemporary pagan, witchcraft-based religion, incorporates a variety of meditation techniques to enhance spiritual growth, develop psychic abilities, and establish a deeper connection with the natural world and the divine. These meditation techniques in Wicca are diverse, drawing from both ancient and modern sources, and offer practitioners a unique and profound way to explore their inner selves and the spiritual realms.

One of the most commonly used meditation techniques in Wicca is guided meditation. This method involves a Wiccan practitioner or leader guiding participants through a visualization process. The guided meditation may take the form of a journey through the elements, a visit to the Wiccan wheel of the year, or an encounter with deities and spirits. Guided meditation serves to deepen one's connection to the Wiccan cosmology, fostering a sense of unity with the natural world and the divine forces that Wiccans worship.

Another meditation technique found in Wicca is mantra meditation. Mantras are repetitive phrases or words chanted or recited silently to focus the mind and induce a meditative state. In Wicca, these mantras often revolve around invoking specific deities, attuning to the elements, or affirming positive intentions. The repetition of these sacred words helps Wiccans attune themselves to specific energies and intentions, fostering a sense of harmony and alignment with their spiritual goals.

Breathwork meditation is another integral practice in Wicca. This technique involves controlled breathing exercises to quiet the mind and facilitate a state of relaxation and heightened awareness. Wiccans often incorporate specific breathing patterns, such as deep belly breathing or rhythmic breathing in their meditative practices. Breathwork meditation not only aids in grounding and centering but also helps Wiccans align their energies with the natural rhythms of the earth. Wicca

also incorporates the use of candles in meditation. Candle meditation involves focusing on the flame of a candle as a focal point to still the mind and enhance concentration. Wiccans believe that fire has a purifying and transformative energy, making it a potent tool for meditation. By gazing at the flame and allowing their thoughts to flow with it, practitioners can achieve a more profound state of meditation and connect with the fire element, one of the essential components of Wiccan spirituality.

Chakra meditation is another technique embraced by some Wiccans, drawing inspiration from Hindu and yogic practices. In this form of meditation, practitioners work with the idea of chakras, which are energy centers aligned along the spine. Wiccans believe that each chakra corresponds to specific aspects of human consciousness and can be harmonized and balanced through meditation. By meditating on these energy centers, Wiccans seek to achieve emotional and spiritual equilibrium, fostering a sense of overall well-being.

An essential aspect of Wicca is its reverence for the natural world, and nature-based meditation techniques play a vital role in Wiccan practice. Forest bathing, or "Shinrin-yoku," is one such technique that involves immersing oneself in nature to connect with the energies of the earth, trees, and wildlife. Wiccans who practice this form of meditation believe it enhances their connection to the natural world, making them more attuned to the cycles of nature and the spirits of the land.

Trance meditation is another unique meditation technique in Wicca. Trance states involve deep relaxation, altered consciousness, and heightened receptivity to spiritual experiences. Wiccans use trance meditation to facilitate direct communication with deities, ancestors, and spirit guides. By inducing a trance-like state through rhythmic drumming, chanting, or dancing, practitioners open themselves to visions, insights, and divine guidance.

In conclusion, Wicca incorporates a diverse array of meditation techniques that serve as powerful tools for spiritual growth, self-discovery, and connection to the natural and supernatural realms. From guided meditation to mantra meditation, breathwork, candle meditation, chakra meditation, nature-based meditation, and trance meditation, these practices allow Wiccans to explore the depths of their consciousness and forge a profound connection with the forces that shape their beliefs and spirituality. Ultimately, these meditation techniques in Wicca empower individuals to walk their spiritual path with clarity, wisdom, and a deep sense of connection to the sacred.

Connecting with the natural world: Nature as a teacher

Wicca, a modern pagan and witchcraft-based religion, places a deep and profound emphasis on the connection with the natural world. Central to Wiccan beliefs is the idea that nature is a teacher, a source of wisdom, and a wellspring of spiritual insight. In this section, we will explore how Wicca celebrates and embraces the teachings of nature, viewing it as not only a physical but also a spiritual and metaphysical teacher.

One of the fundamental principles of Wicca is the veneration of nature as sacred. Wiccans view the natural world as a manifestation of the divine, where every tree, rock, animal, and element is infused with spiritual significance. This perspective allows Wiccans to see nature as a teacher, constantly offering lessons about the cycles of life, the interconnectedness of all living things, and the inherent magic that permeates the world. Through this lens, Wiccans learn to appreciate and respect the Earth as a living entity deserving of reverence and care.

Wicca's connection to nature is deeply rooted in its seasonal festivals, known as Sabbats. These celebrations mark the cycles of the sun and the changing of the seasons, aligning Wiccans with the Earth's natural rhythms. Each Sabbat, such as Beltane, Litha, and Samhain, provides an opportunity to connect with specific aspects of nature and its teachings. For example, Samhain, the festival of the ancestors and the dead, teaches Wiccans about the cycle of life, death, and rebirth, which emphasizes the interconnectedness of all life forms.

The Wheel of the Year, a central concept in Wicca, further underscores the importance of nature as a teacher. This cyclical calendar reflects the changing seasons and their spiritual significance. By observing and celebrating the Wheel of the Year, Wiccans gain a deep understanding of the Earth's natural rhythms and how they correspond to their own spiritual journeys. The lessons of nature are woven into the very fabric of Wiccan practice, guiding practitioners through a continuous cycle of growth, reflection, and renewal.

Wicca also embraces the idea of animism, the belief that all things possess a spirit or consciousness. This animistic perspective allows Wiccans to commune with the spirits of nature, including the spirits of trees, rivers, animals, and even the elements themselves. By establishing a connection with these spirits, Wiccans gain insight, guidance, and wisdom from the natural world. For example, a Wiccan might meditate by a flowing river to commune with the spirit of water, seeking inspiration and emotional healing.

The concept of the "Green Man" is another powerful symbol in Wicca that underscores nature's role as a teacher. The Green Man, often depicted as a face surrounded by leaves and foliage, represents the spirit of the wilderness and the vitality of the natural world. Wiccans revere the Green Man as a symbol of the cyclical nature of life, death, and rebirth. By connecting with this archetype, Wiccans learn to embrace change, transformation, and the eternal renewal of life's cycles.

Nature as a teacher in Wicca also extends to the practice of herbalism. Wiccans have a deep affinity for working with herbs, recognizing them as potent conduits of natural wisdom and healing. The study of herbalism allows Wiccans to learn from the plants themselves, understanding their unique properties, correspondences, and magical uses. Herbs become teachers, offering their knowledge to those who seek to harness their power in spells, rituals, and healing practices.

Furthermore, Wiccans often engage in outdoor rituals and ceremonies, known as "circle casting," which are conducted in natural settings such as forests, meadows, and seashores. These rituals allow practitioners to directly connect with the energies of the land, the elements, and the spirits of nature. By conducting ceremonies in these natural environments, Wiccans deepen their bond with the Earth and draw inspiration from its teachings.

In conclusion, Wicca's profound connection with the natural world makes it a unique and nature-centered spiritual path. Wiccans view nature as not only a physical but also a spiritual teacher, providing valuable lessons about the interconnectedness of all life, the cycles of the seasons, and the inherent magic that permeates the world. Through the Wheel of the Year, animism, the Green Man, herbalism, and outdoor rituals, Wiccans continually seek to learn from and honor the wisdom of nature. In doing so, they cultivate a deep and transformative relationship with the Earth, allowing nature to guide them on their spiritual journeys and inspire a profound sense of reverence for the sacredness of the natural world.

Inner growth and spiritual development through Wiccan practices

Wicca, a contemporary pagan and witchcraft-based religion, offers a rich and profound path for inner growth and spiritual development. Rooted in the veneration of nature and the worship of a diverse pantheon of deities, Wiccan practices are designed to facilitate personal transformation, deepen one's connection with the divine, and foster a harmonious relationship with the natural world. In this section, we will explore how Wiccan rituals, traditions, and beliefs contribute to inner growth and spiritual development.

Central to Wicca is the practice of ritual magic, which serves as a powerful tool for personal transformation. Rituals are carefully structured and symbolic acts performed to achieve specific spiritual or magical goals. These rituals frequently include the use of candles, herbs, crystals, incense, and other magical tools. Through the repetition of these rites, Wiccans develop discipline, focus, and a heightened sense of self-awareness. By participating in rituals that align with their intentions, practitioners can bring about positive change in their lives, addressing issues such as self-confidence, healing, and personal empowerment.

Wiccan rituals also promote mindfulness and presence in the moment. During a ritual, participants are encouraged to be fully engaged in the experience, leaving behind distractions and worries from the outside world. This mindful approach helps individuals develop a deeper connection with their inner selves and the energies they are working with. It fosters a sense of unity with the divine, as Wiccans believe that they are co-creating their reality with the gods and goddesses they invoke.

One of the core principles of Wicca is the belief in the duality of the divine, often represented as the God and Goddess. This dualistic perspective allows Wiccans to explore the complementary aspects of the human psyche and the universe. Through rituals that honor both the God and Goddess, practitioners gain a greater understanding of the balance between light and dark, masculine and feminine, and life and death. This recognition of duality encourages personal growth by acknowledging the complexity of human nature and the world we inhabit. Wicca's emphasis on the cycles of nature also contributes to inner growth and spiritual development. Wiccans celebrate the changing seasons and the cycles of the moon, which mirror the rhythms of life, death, and rebirth. By attuning themselves to these natural cycles, practitioners learn to embrace change, transition, and personal transformation. The Wheel of the Year, a central concept in Wicca, provides a framework for reflecting on one's own life journey and spiritual evolution.

Another significant aspect of Wiccan practice is the study of symbolism and correspondences. Wiccans often work with a variety of symbols, colors, and elements that have specific meanings and associations. This practice enhances their ability to interpret the language of the universe and gain insight into the spiritual realms. By delving into symbolism, Wiccans deepen their understanding of the hidden aspects of reality and their own inner symbolism, which can lead to profound personal insights and spiritual growth.

Wiccan ethics and values also play a pivotal role in inner growth. The Wiccan Rede, a moral guideline that advises, "An it harm none, do what ye will," promotes responsible and ethical behavior. This principle encourages practitioners to consider the consequences of their actions and decisions, fostering personal responsibility and self-awareness. Through the application of these ethical principles, Wiccans cultivate a sense of integrity, empathy, and compassion, leading to personal growth and a greater connection with the spiritual dimensions of life.

Meditation is another essential component of Wiccan practice that contributes to inner growth and spiritual development. Wiccans use meditation to quiet the mind, focus their intention, and connect with the divine. Meditation allows practitioners to explore the depths of their consciousness, encounter spirit guides and deities, and gain profound insights into their personal spiritual path. It fosters self-reflection, emotional healing, and spiritual alignment, facilitating personal growth on multiple levels.

Furthermore, Wicca's emphasis on the importance of personal experience and direct connection with the divine encourages practitioners to trust their intuition and inner wisdom. Unlike some religious traditions that rely heavily on dogma and religious authorities, Wicca empowers individuals to forge their unique spiritual paths. This freedom allows for personal growth as individuals explore their beliefs, experiment with different practices, and develop a deeper connection with the divine that is deeply rooted in their own experiences.

In conclusion, Wicca provides a holistic and transformative framework for inner growth and spiritual development. Through rituals, mindfulness, duality, natural cycles, symbolism, ethical principles, meditation, and personal empowerment, Wiccans embark on a journey of self-discovery and spiritual evolution. Wiccan practices encourage individuals to connect with their inner selves, the divine, and the natural world, fostering personal growth, self-awareness, and a more profound understanding of the interconnectedness of all life. As Wiccans honor the sacred within themselves and in the world around them, they continue to evolve spiritually, nurturing a profound and enduring connection with the divine.

The concept of the higher self in Wicca

Wicca, a contemporary pagan and witchcraft-based religion, places a strong emphasis on personal spirituality and self-discovery. One of the central and profound concepts in Wicca is the notion of the "Higher Self." This concept, which is central to Wiccan belief and practice, represents an individual's true, divine, and enlightened nature. In this section, we will explore the concept of the Higher Self in Wicca, its significance, and how it informs the spiritual journey of Wiccan practitioners.

The Higher Self in Wicca is often described as the most authentic and pure aspect of an individual's consciousness. It is the part of one's self that is intimately connected to the divine, the universal energies, and the spiritual realms. Wiccans believe that every person possesses a Higher Self, although it may remain largely dormant or obscured by the distractions and challenges of everyday life. Discovering and connecting with the Higher Self is considered a fundamental element of spiritual growth and enlightenment in Wicca.

One of the key teachings in Wicca is the idea that the material world, while important, is not the ultimate reality. The Higher Self is a metaphor for a more profound, spiritual aspect of life that exists outside the bounds of the material world. According to Wiccan belief, people can access their inner wisdom, gain spiritual insights, and receive the divine guidance required for their own and magick's development by acknowledging and connecting with their Higher Self.

To connect with the Higher Self, Wiccans often engage in various spiritual practices and rituals. Meditation is a particularly essential tool for this purpose. Through meditation, practitioners quiet the mind, still the ego, and create a space for the Higher Self to emerge. In this state of deep inner awareness, individuals can gain insights into their true purpose, desires, and the path to self-realization. Meditation also facilitates direct communication with the Higher Self, allowing Wiccans to seek guidance, receive inspiration, and experience moments of profound spiritual revelation.

Another integral aspect of connecting with the Higher Self in Wicca is the practice of visualization. Visualization techniques involve creating mental images or "seeing with the mind's eye" to connect with the divine, access inner wisdom, and manifest one's desires. Wiccans often use visualization to communicate with their Higher Selves, envision their spiritual goals, and work magic. This process allows practitioners to align their intentions with their Higher Self's wisdom and power, creating a harmonious flow of energy and intent.

The concept of the Higher Self also influences the ethical and moral framework of Wicca. Wiccans believe that the Higher Self is inherently attuned to love, compassion, and ethical behavior. As individuals connect more deeply with their Higher Selves, they naturally develop a sense of empathy, responsibility, and ethical consciousness. The Wiccan Rede, which advises, "An it harm none, do what ye will," reflects this ethical perspective, emphasizing the importance of aligning one's actions with the higher principles of love and harmlessness.

The concept of the Higher Self is closely intertwined with the idea of personal empowerment in Wicca. Wiccan practitioners believe that by connecting with their Higher Selves, they gain access to a wellspring of inner strength, confidence, and self-acceptance. This self-empowerment enables them to overcome challenges, manifest their desires, and lead more fulfilling lives. Through rituals, spells, and magical workings, Wiccans harness the energy of their Higher Selves to effect positive change in the world and within themselves.

In Wiccan rituals, the invocation and communion with the Higher Self is a central element. During ceremonies, practitioners often call upon their Higher Selves, as well as the deities and spirits they work with, to empower their magical workings and spiritual endeavors. This connection with the Higher Self reinforces the belief that one's true, divine nature is an integral part of the sacred work being performed.

Furthermore, the concept of the Higher Self in Wicca plays a crucial role in the development of a practitioner's personal belief system. Wicca is a highly individualized and eclectic religion, with an array of beliefs and practices. As Wiccans connect with their Higher Selves, they are encouraged to explore their unique spiritual path, seeking personal insights and revelations. This process allows individuals to develop their own interpretations of Wiccan theology and incorporate elements that resonate most deeply with their Higher Selves.

In conclusion, the concept of the Higher Self in Wicca is a cornerstone of spiritual growth and self-discovery. It represents the most authentic and divine aspect of an individual's consciousness, serving as a source of inner wisdom, guidance, and empowerment. Through meditation, visualization, ethical principles, personal empowerment, and ritual practice, Wiccans cultivate a profound connection with their Higher Selves, enhancing their spiritual journey and deepening their understanding of the sacred. The Higher Self in Wicca is not only a concept but a dynamic and transformative force that empowers individuals to align with their true nature and experience the depths of their spiritual potential.

CHAPTER VI

Wiccan Ethics and Social Responsibility

Wicca and the environment: Eco-spirituality

Wicca, a contemporary pagan and witchcraft-based religion, is deeply rooted in the reverence and veneration of the natural world. This spiritual tradition places a strong emphasis on the interconnectedness of all life forms and views the environment as sacred. This eco- spiritual perspective sets Wicca apart from many mainstream religions and fosters a profound relationship between practitioners and the natural world. In this section, we will explore how Wicca's eco-spirituality is manifested in its beliefs, practices, and ethical principles, and how it contributes to the broader conversation about environmental sustainability and conservation.

Central to Wicca's eco-spirituality is the belief in the sacredness of nature. Wiccans see the Earth as a living entity deserving of reverence and care. They regard natural landscapes, such as forests, meadows, and bodies of water, as sacred spaces where they can connect with the divine. This belief is reflected in Wiccan rituals and ceremonies, which are often conducted outdoors in natural settings to honor the land and the elements. By celebrating the cycles of the seasons and the phases of the moon, Wiccans align themselves with the rhythms of nature and deepen their spiritual connection to the environment.

The Wheel of the Year, a central concept in Wicca, further underscores the importance of eco-spirituality. This cyclical calendar marks the changing seasons and the associated Sabbats or festivals. Each Sabbat, such as Imbolc, Beltane, and Mabon, provides an opportunity for Wiccans to attune themselves to the natural world and its teachings. For example, Beltane, a celebration of fertility and the abundance of life, encourages practitioners to reflect on the Earth's capacity for growth and renewal, inspiring them to nurture their own spiritual and personal growth.

The concept of animism, the belief that all things possess a spirit or consciousness, is integral to Wicca's eco-spirituality. Wiccans believe that every plant, animal, rock, and element has its own spirit, and they interact with these spirits in their rituals and daily lives. This perspective fosters a deep respect for the interconnectedness of all living beings and encourages practitioners to live in harmony with nature. For example, when Wiccans harvest herbs for magical or medicinal purposes, they ask for permission from the plant spirits and offer gratitude for their gifts, demonstrating a profound reverence for the environment.

Wicca's ethical principles also reflect its commitment to eco-spirituality. The Wiccan Rede, a moral guideline that advises, "An it harm none, do what ye will," emphasizes the importance of ethical behavior and harmlessness in all actions. This principle extends to the treatment of the environment and all its inhabitants. Wiccans believe that harming the Earth or its creatures is a violation of the Rede and goes against the principles of eco-spirituality. This ethical perspective encourages environmental stewardship, conservation efforts, and sustainable living practices among Wiccans.

Wiccan magical practices are often aligned with eco-spirituality. Many Wiccans work magic to manifest positive change in the world, including efforts to protect and heal the environment. For example, environmental activists within the Wiccan community may conduct magical workings to raise awareness about environmental issues, empower conservation efforts, or promote sustainable practices. Through their magic, Wiccans seek to harness the natural energies of the Earth and the elements to create a positive impact on the environment.

Furthermore, Wicca encourages a deep sense of personal responsibility for the environment. Wiccans believe that every individual has a role to play in preserving and protecting the Earth. This sense of responsibility is not limited to ritual or magical practices but extends to everyday actions and choices. Wiccans often embrace sustainable living practices, such as recycling, reducing waste, conserving energy, and supporting eco-friendly initiatives. They view these actions as an integral part of their commitment to eco-spirituality and their role as stewards of the Earth.

Wicca's eco-spirituality also has implications for the broader environmental movement. By fostering a deep connection with the natural world and a sense of responsibility for its well-being, Wicca contributes to the growing awareness of environmental issues and the importance of conservation efforts. Wiccans are often advocates for sustainable living, renewable energy sources, and the protection of endangered species and ecosystems. Their eco-spiritual perspective offers a unique and holistic approach to environmentalism, emphasizing not only physical conservation but also the spiritual and emotional connection to the Earth.

In conclusion, Wicca's eco-spirituality is a profound and transformative aspect of this contemporary pagan tradition. It celebrates the sacredness of nature, fosters a deep reverence for the environment, and promotes ethical principles that encourage responsible stewardship of the Earth. Wiccans' rituals, beliefs, magical practices, and personal actions all reflect their commitment to eco-spirituality and their belief in the interconnectedness of all life forms. As Wiccans continue to honor the natural world and its teachings, they contribute to a broader dialogue on environmental sustainability and conservation, offering a spiritual perspective that can inspire positive change and greater harmony with the Earth.

Wiccan perspectives on social justice and inclusivity

Wicca, a modern pagan and witchcraft-based religion, holds a unique perspective on social justice and inclusivity. Rooted in principles of personal empowerment, ethical conduct, and reverence for nature, Wicca advocates for a world where individuals are free to express their true selves and where justice and equality prevail. In this section, we will explore Wiccan perspectives on social justice, inclusivity, and the ways in which this spiritual tradition seeks to promote a more equitable and compassionate society.

Central to Wicca's perspective on social justice is the belief in the importance of individual autonomy and personal responsibility. Wicca teaches that each person is responsible for their own actions, and this principle extends to the realm of social justice. Wiccans believe that individuals must take responsibility for their beliefs, actions, and contributions to society. This perspective encourages Wiccans to engage in self-reflection and self-improvement, recognizing that personal growth is an essential step toward creating a just and inclusive world.

The ethical principles of Wicca, as embodied in the Wiccan Rede, "An it harm none, do what ye will," emphasize the importance of ethical conduct and harmlessness in all actions. This moral guideline encourages Wiccans to consider the consequences of their actions on others and the world around them. In the context of social justice, the Wiccan Rede promotes the idea that individuals should strive to avoid causing harm, discrimination, or injustice to others. It underscores the importance of empathy, compassion, and ethical behavior in all interactions, contributing to a more inclusive and equitable society.

Wicca's belief in the sacredness of all life and the interconnectedness of all beings also informs its perspective on social justice. Wiccans view the natural world and all living creatures as sacred, recognizing that every being has inherent worth and value. This perspective fosters a deep respect for diversity and inclusivity, as Wiccans believe that all individuals, regardless of their background, identity, or beliefs, should be treated with respect and dignity. In Wiccan rituals and ceremonies, this reverence for diversity is often reflected in the acknowledgment and celebration of different deities and spiritual traditions.

Furthermore, Wicca's emphasis on the balance of masculine and feminine energies contributes to its perspective on social justice and inclusivity. Wiccans believe in the equality of genders and celebrate the divine in both male and female forms. This gender equality aligns with the broader goals of social justice, advocating for equal rights and opportunities for all genders. Wiccans often reject patriarchal and discriminatory practices, emphasizing the importance of respecting and empowering individuals of all genders and gender identities.

Wicca's commitment to environmental stewardship and the preservation of the natural world also has implications for social justice. Wiccans recognize that environmental degradation disproportionately affects marginalized communities and future generations. As a result, they view environmental activism and sustainability as essential components of social justice. Wiccans often advocate for eco-friendly practices, renewable energy sources, and the protection of ecosystems as part of their commitment to creating a more equitable and sustainable world.

Wicca's perspective on social justice also extends to the broader issues of human rights and social equality. Many Wiccans are advocates for social justice causes, including LGBTQ+ rights, racial equality, women's rights, and indigenous rights. Wiccans view these causes as aligned with their spiritual principles of inclusivity, diversity, and ethical conduct. They often participate in social justice movements, protests, and awareness campaigns, working toward a world where all individuals are treated with fairness and respect.

Inclusivity is a core value in Wicca, and many Wiccan covens and communities strive to create welcoming and diverse spaces for individuals of all backgrounds. Discrimination or exclusion based on race, gender, sexual orientation, or any other characteristic is often viewed as antithetical to Wiccan principles. In Wiccan circles, individuals are encouraged to express their true selves and celebrate their uniqueness. This perspective fosters a sense of belonging and acceptance that can be transformative for those who have experienced marginalization or discrimination in other aspects of their lives.

In conclusion, Wicca's perspectives on social justice and inclusivity are deeply rooted in its principles of personal empowerment, ethical conduct, reverence for nature, and respect for diversity. Wiccans believe in the importance of individual responsibility, harmlessness, and empathy in creating a more just and inclusive society. They advocate for equality, gender equity, environmental sustainability, and human rights, and often engage in social justice activism to promote these values. In Wiccan communities, inclusivity and diversity are celebrated, creating spaces where individuals from all backgrounds can find acceptance and support. Wicca's unique spiritual perspective contributes to the broader conversation about social justice, offering insights and principles that can inspire positive change and greater equity in the world.

Community involvement and activism in the Wiccan community

The Wiccan community, like many other religious and spiritual groups, places a strong emphasis on community involvement and activism. Rooted in principles of empowerment, ethical responsibility, and reverence for nature, Wiccans believe that their spiritual path extends beyond personal growth and into the broader world. In this section, we will explore the ways in which community involvement and activism are integral to the Wiccan tradition, examining the motivations behind such engagement and the impact it has on both the Wiccan community and society at large.

Central to the Wiccan tradition is the belief in personal empowerment and the capacity for positive change. Wiccans often view their spiritual path as a journey of self-discovery and self-empowerment, and this empowerment extends to their role in the community and society. Many Wiccans feel a deep sense of responsibility to use their knowledge, skills, and resources to effect positive change in the world. This motivation is grounded in the belief that individuals have the power to make a difference and create a more just and sustainable society. Wiccans are often drawn to social and environmental causes that align with their spiritual values. Given Wicca's reverence for nature and its commitment to ethical conduct, environmental activism is a common focus of community involvement. Many Wiccans are advocates for conservation, sustainable living, and the protection of natural ecosystems. They view their connection to the Earth as a sacred bond and feel a moral obligation to protect and preserve the environment for future generations.

Social justice issues also resonate deeply with the Wiccan community. Wiccans often embrace causes related to LGBTQ+ rights, racial equality, women's rights, indigenous rights, and other social justice movements. These causes align with Wicca's principles of inclusivity, diversity, and harmlessness. Wiccans view discrimination, prejudice, and inequality as antithetical to their spiritual beliefs and feel compelled to work toward a more equitable and just society.

Community involvement and activism take various forms within the Wiccan community. Many Wiccans engage in grassroots activism, participating in protests, marches, and awareness campaigns to advocate for social and environmental causes. They see these activities as an extension of their spiritual values and a way to effect change on a societal level. Wiccan activists often draw on their spiritual practices, such as meditation, ritual, and spellwork, to empower their efforts and manifest positive outcomes.

Wiccans also contribute to their communities through volunteer work and charitable activities. Many Wiccan covens and groups organize community service projects, such as food drives, environmental cleanups, and fundraisers for charitable organizations. This involvement reflects the Wiccan principle of "harm none" and emphasizes the importance of giving back to the community. It also serves as a way for Wiccans to demonstrate the positive impact of their spiritual beliefs on society.

Inclusivity and support are key elements of the Wiccan community's approach to community involvement.

Wiccan covens and groups often provide a welcoming and inclusive space for individuals from diverse backgrounds and beliefs. This sense of belonging and acceptance can be transformative for those who have experienced marginalization or discrimination in other aspects of their lives. Wiccan communities frequently offer support and resources to those in need, further exemplifying their commitment to ethical responsibility and community care.

Furthermore, Wiccan community involvement often extends to interfaith and interreligious dialogues. Wiccans recognize the importance of fostering understanding and cooperation among different spiritual and religious traditions. They actively engage in conversations with representatives of other faiths, seeking common ground and shared values. This interfaith dialogue contributes to a broader sense of unity and collaboration within the broader religious and spiritual landscape.

The impact of community involvement and activism within the Wiccan community is multifaceted. On an individual level, it allows Wiccans to live out their spiritual values in a tangible and meaningful way. It provides a sense of purpose and fulfillment, as individuals actively work toward the betterment of society and the environment. Community involvement also strengthens the bonds between Wiccans, fostering a sense of unity and shared purpose within the community.

On a societal level, Wiccan activism and community involvement contribute to positive change and awareness of important issues. Wiccans are often at the forefront of environmental and social justice movements, advocating for policies and practices that promote sustainability, equality, and justice. Their commitment to ethical conduct and inclusivity sets an example for others and encourages a broader conversation about the interconnectedness of all life forms and the importance of social and environmental responsibility.

In conclusion, community involvement and activism are integral aspects of the Wiccan tradition, reflecting the spiritual values of empowerment, ethical responsibility, and reverence for nature. Wiccans are motivated to engage with social and environmental causes that align with their beliefs, seeking to create a more just, inclusive, and sustainable society. Through grassroots activism, volunteer work, interfaith dialogues, and support for marginalized communities, Wiccans contribute to positive change on both individual and societal levels. Their involvement demonstrates the transformative power of spirituality when harnessed for the greater good, inspiring others to take action and make a difference in the world.

Ethical considerations in teaching and sharing Wiccan knowledge

Wicca, a contemporary pagan and witchcraft-based religion, places a strong emphasis on ethical conduct, personal responsibility, and the careful transmission of knowledge. Within the Wiccan community, there is a long-standing tradition of teaching and sharing spiritual wisdom and practices. However, this process comes with ethical considerations that are deeply rooted in the Wiccan principles of harmlessness, respect for free will, and the preservation of the sacred mysteries. In this section, we will explore the ethical considerations that Wiccans take into account when teaching and sharing their knowledge within the community.

One of the fundamental ethical principles in Wicca is the concept of "harm none." This principle, often encapsulated in the Wiccan Rede as "An it harm none, do what ye will," underscores the importance of avoiding harm to others in one's actions and decisions. When teaching and sharing Wiccan knowledge, practitioners must apply this principle by ensuring that their teachings do not lead to harm or exploitation. This ethical consideration extends to the practice of magic, as Wiccans believe that magical workings should be conducted responsibly and ethically, with the intention of bringing about positive change without causing harm to others.

Respect for free will is another crucial ethical consideration in Wiccan teaching. Wiccans hold a strong belief in the autonomy of individuals and the importance of personal choice in matters of spirituality. When sharing their knowledge, Wiccans emphasize the importance of informed consent and the freedom for individuals to explore their spiritual paths without coercion or manipulation. This respect for free will also applies to the practice of magic, as Wiccans do not use their skills to interfere with the choices or lives of others without their explicit consent.

Secrecy and the preservation of the sacred mysteries are significant ethical considerations in Wiccan teaching. Wicca is known for its initiatory traditions, where practitioners are initiated into the mysteries of the tradition through a formal process. These mysteries are often safeguarded through oaths of secrecy, and Wiccans are bound by a sense of honor and ethical responsibility to protect the integrity of their tradition. When teaching, Wiccans must carefully balance the desire to share knowledge with the need to uphold the sacredness and confidentiality of the tradition's mysteries.

Inclusivity and diversity are ethical considerations that have gained prominence in recent years within the Wiccan community. Many Wiccans recognize the importance of creating inclusive and welcoming spaces for individuals from diverse backgrounds, identities, and belief systems. When teaching and sharing Wiccan knowledge, practitioners must be mindful of the potential for exclusivity or cultural appropriation. Ethical Wiccan teachers strive to respect and honor the cultural origins of their practices, avoid cultural appropriation, and promote diversity and inclusivity within the community.

Transparency and accountability are also essential ethical considerations in Wiccan teaching. Practitioners who take on the role of teachers or mentors must be transparent about their qualifications, experience, and intentions. They should provide clear guidelines for their students, including expectations, boundaries, and the nature of the teachings. Ethical teachers are accountable for their actions and should be open to feedback and constructive criticism from their students and the wider community.

The issue of commercialization and the ethical use of Wiccan knowledge for financial gain is another concern within the community. While it is acceptable for Wiccan teachers to charge fees for their time and resources, ethical considerations come into play when profit becomes the primary motivation. Ethical teachers strike a balance between offering their knowledge for a fair exchange and ensuring that the spiritual path remains accessible to those who may not have the financial means to pay for expensive courses or materials.

Integrity and honesty are foundational ethical principles in Wicca. Wiccans are encouraged to live authentically, with integrity and honesty in all aspects of their lives. When teaching and sharing Wiccan knowledge, practitioners must model these virtues and emphasize their importance to their students. Ethical teachers also maintain the integrity of their tradition and teachings by refraining from misrepresenting their lineage, qualifications, or the nature of their practices.

In conclusion, ethical considerations play a vital role in the teaching and sharing of Wiccan knowledge within the community. Wiccans are guided by principles of harmlessness, respect for free will, and the preservation of sacred mysteries. They strive to create inclusive and diverse spaces, practice transparency and accountability, and uphold the values of integrity and honesty. These ethical considerations ensure that the transmission of Wiccan knowledge is conducted responsibly and in alignment with the core principles of the tradition. By upholding these ethical standards, Wiccans continue to foster a community where individuals can explore their spiritual paths with integrity, respect, and a commitment to the highest ethical standards.

Building bridges with other spiritual traditions

Wicca, a contemporary pagan and witchcraft-based religion, has a rich history of embracing diversity and inclusivity, not only within its own community but also in building bridges with other spiritual traditions. Despite its distinct beliefs and practices, Wicca encourages interfaith dialogue, mutual understanding, and cooperation with practitioners of various spiritual paths. In this section, we will explore the ways in which Wiccans seek to build bridges with other spiritual traditions, the motivations behind such efforts, and the benefits of fostering connections with a broader spiritual community.

One of the core principles of Wicca is the belief in the interconnectedness of all life and the recognition of the divine in various forms. Wiccans often express a reverence for nature and the sacredness of the Earth, which resonates with many indigenous and earth-centered spiritual traditions. This common ground forms a natural bridge between Wicca and other belief systems that share a deep connection to the natural world. Wiccans often engage in interfaith dialogue with representatives of these traditions, seeking to learn from their practices, share insights, and promote mutual respect for the environment.

The Wiccan perspective on gender equality and the veneration of both the masculine and feminine aspects of the divine aligns with the values of many feminist and women-centered spiritual traditions. Wicca's emphasis on the balance of energies, as exemplified in the concept of the God and Goddess, fosters a sense of unity and commonality with spiritual paths that celebrate the divine feminine. Wiccans often collaborate with practitioners of these traditions to promote gender equality and support women's empowerment.

Wiccans also engage in interfaith dialogue with representatives of other pagan and polytheistic traditions. While each tradition may have its unique pantheon of deities, there is often a shared recognition of the multiplicity of divine beings. This commonality provides an opportunity for practitioners of different traditions to discuss theology, mythology, and the nature of deity. Through these conversations, bridges are built, and a deeper understanding of the diversity of pagan and polytheistic beliefs emerges.

Eclecticism is a hallmark of modern Wicca, and many Wiccans draw inspiration from a wide range of spiritual traditions. This eclecticism often leads to the integration of elements from other belief systems into Wiccan practice. For example, some Wiccans incorporate elements of Eastern spirituality, such as meditation techniques or concepts of energy work, into their rituals and magical practices. This willingness to adapt and incorporate ideas from other traditions demonstrates a commitment to openness and a desire to learn from a diverse range of spiritual sources.

The experience of religious discrimination and misunderstanding has motivated many Wiccans to actively build bridges with other spiritual traditions. Wiccans have faced prejudice and bias from mainstream religions and society, leading them to empathize with practitioners of other minority religions and belief systems. This shared experience of religious discrimination creates a common ground for dialogue and collaboration with other marginalized religious groups, fostering a sense of solidarity and mutual support.

Interfaith and inter-spiritual gatherings and events provide opportunities for Wiccans to connect with practitioners of various spiritual traditions. These gatherings often focus on shared values, such as peace, tolerance, and environmental stewardship. By participating in these events, Wiccans not only build bridges with other traditions but also demonstrate their commitment to promoting peace and understanding among diverse spiritual communities.

The benefits of building bridges with other spiritual traditions in Wicca are numerous. First and foremost, it promotes a sense of unity and cooperation among practitioners of different belief systems. By fostering understanding and mutual respect, these efforts contribute to a more inclusive and tolerant spiritual landscape. Wiccans also gain valuable insights and perspectives from other traditions, enriching their own spiritual practices and deepening their understanding of the broader spiritual tapestry.

Building bridges with other traditions also strengthens the voice of the pagan and earth-centered spiritual communities in the wider world. By collaborating with practitioners of other paths, Wiccans can work together on common goals, such as environmental conservation, religious freedom advocacy, and social justice initiatives. This collective effort amplifies their impact and raises awareness of pagan and earth-centered spiritual traditions on a global scale.

In conclusion, building bridges with other spiritual traditions is a fundamental aspect of Wicca's commitment to diversity, inclusivity, and cooperation. Wiccans seek to find common ground with practitioners of various beliefs, recognizing the interconnectedness of all spiritual paths. Through interfaith dialogue, collaboration, and the sharing of insights, Wiccans contribute to a more inclusive and harmonious spiritual landscape. By embracing the opportunity to learn from and connect with other traditions, Wiccans enrich their own spiritual journeys and promote a broader sense of unity and understanding among diverse spiritual communities.

CHAPTER VII

Challenges and Controversies

Addressing misconceptions and stereotypes about Wicca

Wicca, a contemporary pagan and witchcraft-based religion, has long been the subject of misconceptions and stereotypes in popular culture and mainstream society. These misunderstandings often arise from misinformation, lack of exposure, and the portrayal of Wicca in media and literature. In this section, we will explore some of the most common misconceptions and stereotypes about Wicca, provide accurate information to address them, and discuss the importance of dispelling these myths for a more informed and respectful understanding of the religion.

One of the most prevalent misconceptions about Wicca is that it is synonymous with Satanism or devil worship. This misconception likely stems from the historical association of witchcraft with heresy in Christian Europe. However, Wicca has no connection to Satanism. Wiccans do not believe in Satan, as their religious framework revolves around the veneration of nature, the worship of a dual divinity often referred to as the God and Goddess, and the practice of ethical principles, such as the Wiccan Rede, which emphasizes harmlessness and ethical conduct. Another common misconception is that Wicca is a "dark" or malevolent religion focused on hexes, curses, and harmful magic. In reality, Wicca promotes ethical magic and spellwork that adheres to the principle of "harm none." Wiccans believe in the law of return, often referred to as the Threefold Law, which states that any energy or intention put into the world, whether positive or negative, will come back to the sender threefold. This belief reinforces the importance of responsible and benevolent magical practices.

Wicca is often portrayed in the media as a secretive and exclusive cult, leading to the misconception that it is inaccessible to outsiders or that it involves secretive and dangerous rituals. While some Wiccan traditions do have initiatory practices and oaths of secrecy, many Wiccans are open to sharing information about their beliefs and practices. There are numerous books, websites, and public events where individuals interested in Wicca can learn about the religion in an open and respectful manner. Additionally, the vast majority of Wiccan rituals are not secretive or dangerous but rather focused on worship, celebration of nature's cycles, and personal growth.

The misconception that Wicca is solely a religion for women or that it excludes men is another common stereotype. In reality, Wicca is an inclusive and gender-balanced tradition that celebrates both the masculine and feminine aspects of the divine. While some Wiccans may choose to focus on one aspect of the divine in their personal practice, the religion as a whole values the balance of masculine and feminine energies and welcomes individuals of all genders and gender identities.

Misconceptions about Wiccan morality also abound, with some mistakenly believing that Wicca lacks ethical guidelines or that it condones immoral behavior. In fact, Wicca places a strong emphasis on ethical conduct, encapsulated in the Wiccan Rede, which advises, "An it harm none, do what ye will." This principle underscores the importance of avoiding harm to others and promoting positive actions and intentions. Many Wiccans prioritize living ethically, practicing compassion, and being responsible for their actions.

The stereotype of Wicca as a "fad" or "trendy" religion is another misconception. While interest in Wicca and other forms of modern paganism has grown in recent decades, the religion itself has deep roots and a rich history. Wicca emerged in the mid-20th century but drew inspiration from earlier witchcraft traditions, folklore, and ceremonial magic. Many Wiccans are committed to their spiritual path, and their beliefs and practices are grounded in a profound connection to nature and the sacred.

Addressing these misconceptions and stereotypes about Wicca is essential for several reasons. First and foremost, dispelling these myths promotes religious tolerance and understanding. Stereotypes and misunderstandings can lead to discrimination, bias, and unfair treatment of Wiccans and other pagan practitioners. By providing accurate information, we can foster a more inclusive and respectful society where individuals are free to practice their faith without fear of prejudice or discrimination.

Additionally, addressing misconceptions about Wicca encourages open dialogue and productive conversations about spirituality and religion. When individuals are armed with accurate information, they can engage in informed discussions, ask questions, and seek to understand different belief systems. This promotes a more tolerant and diverse society where people of all faiths can coexist harmoniously.

In conclusion, Wicca, like many religions, has been subject to misconceptions and stereotypes that do not accurately represent its beliefs and practices. Addressing these misconceptions is vital for promoting religious tolerance, understanding, and open dialogue. Wiccans do not worship Satan, engage in malevolent magic, or exclude individuals based on gender. Instead, they adhere to ethical principles, celebrate the balance of masculine and feminine energies, and welcome individuals of all backgrounds and identities. By dispelling these myths, we can create a more informed and respectful society where individuals are free to practice their faith without fear of discrimination or bias.

Ethical dilemmas within the Wiccan community: Secrecy, ethics of initiation, and conflicts

The Wiccan community, like any religious or spiritual tradition, grapples with its own set of ethical dilemmas. These dilemmas can be particularly complex due to Wicca's emphasis on personal autonomy, ethical responsibility, and the preservation of sacred mysteries. In this section, we will explore three primary ethical dilemmas within the Wiccan community: secrecy, ethics of initiation, and conflicts among practitioners. These dilemmas reflect the intricate balance between preserving tradition and fostering a culture of openness and inclusivity.

Secrecy is one of the most notable ethical dilemmas within the Wiccan community. Many Wiccan traditions have a strong emphasis on secrecy, which is rooted in the historical persecution of witches and the desire to protect the integrity of the tradition's teachings and practices. Initiates often take oaths of secrecy to safeguard the sacred mysteries of their tradition. While this secrecy has helped protect Wiccans from persecution and preserve the integrity of the tradition, it can also raise ethical questions about transparency and accessibility.

On one hand, the preservation of secrecy is seen as essential to protect the tradition's integrity and to ensure that its practices are passed down with the utmost respect and care. Secrecy can also create a sense of reverence and ritual significance, enhancing the spiritual experience for practitioners. In many initiatory Wiccan traditions, the revelation of certain teachings and practices is considered a sacred and transformative experience.

On the other hand, the culture of secrecy can be seen as exclusive and potentially alienating to those who are curious about Wicca or interested in learning about the tradition. It can perpetuate the stereotype that Wicca is secretive or clandestine, which may lead to misunderstandings and misconceptions about the religion. Moreover, in an age of information sharing and openness, some argue that strict secrecy may hinder the growth of Wicca and its ability to adapt to modern times.

The ethics of initiation present another ethical dilemma within the Wiccan community. Initiation is a significant and often sacred rite of passage in many Wiccan traditions. It is considered a formal induction into the tradition, a spiritual awakening, and a commitment to the path. Initiates take oaths to honor and uphold the tradition's teachings, ethics, and practices. While initiation is deeply meaningful for many Wiccans, it raises ethical questions about consent and the potential for abuse of power.

Initiation ceremonies are typically conducted by more experienced practitioners, known as priests or priestesses, who serve as mentors and guides to the initiates. This mentorship relationship carries a significant responsibility, as the mentors are entrusted with the spiritual development and well-being of the initiates. Ethical dilemmas can arise when this power dynamic is abused, leading to situations where initiates feel coerced, manipulated, or taken advantage of.

To address this ethical dilemma, some Wiccan traditions emphasize the importance of informed consent and autonomy in the initiation process. Initiates are encouraged to ask questions, understand the commitments they are making, and have the freedom to decline initiation if they have doubts or reservations.

Ethical Wiccan mentors strive to maintain clear boundaries and prioritize the well-being and autonomy of their initiates. They see the initiation as a sacred pact between equals, built on trust and mutual respect.

Conflicts among practitioners are a third ethical dilemma within the Wiccan community. Like any religious or spiritual tradition, Wicca is not immune to interpersonal conflicts, disagreements, and disputes. These conflicts can arise from differences in beliefs, personalities, leadership styles, or interpretations of Wiccan teachings and ethics. While conflicts are a natural part of any community, they present ethical challenges in a tradition that values harmony, respect, and cooperation.

Wiccans often seek to resolve conflicts through open communication, mediation, and a commitment to ethical behavior. The principle of "harm none" is frequently invoked as a guideline for resolving disputes, emphasizing the importance of finding non-harmful and ethical solutions. However, conflicts can still lead to ethical dilemmas when they are not effectively addressed, potentially causing harm to individuals and the community as a whole.

In some cases, conflicts within the Wiccan community may result in the exclusion or ostracism of individuals or groups. This raises ethical questions about fairness, inclusivity, and the potential for discrimination. Wicca places a strong emphasis on inclusivity and the celebration of diversity, which can be challenged when conflicts lead to divisions or exclusions within the community.

Addressing conflicts and ethical dilemmas within the Wiccan community requires a commitment to ethical conduct, open communication, and a willingness to engage in difficult conversations. Some Wiccans emphasize the importance of community-building practices, such as clear codes of conduct, conflict resolution processes, and regular check-ins to ensure that ethical issues are addressed promptly and constructively.

In conclusion, the Wiccan community, like any religious or spiritual tradition, faces ethical dilemmas related to secrecy, the ethics of initiation, and conflicts among practitioners. These dilemmas reflect the complex balance between preserving tradition and fostering a culture of openness and inclusivity. Wiccans grapple with these dilemmas by emphasizing informed consent in initiation, striving for transparency, and promoting ethical behavior and conflict resolution within the community. By addressing these ethical challenges with mindfulness and integrity, Wiccans work to maintain the ethical principles and values that underpin their spiritual tradition while navigating the complexities of the modern world.

The future of Wiccan philosophy and ethics: Evolving perspectives

Wicca, a modern pagan and witchcraft-based religion, has evolved significantly since its emergence in the mid-20th century. As the Wiccan community continues to grow and adapt to the changing world, its philosophy and ethics have also undergone transformations. In this section, we will explore the future of Wiccan philosophy and ethics, examining how evolving perspectives are shaping the tradition, fostering inclusivity, and addressing contemporary ethical challenges.

One notable trend in the evolution of Wiccan philosophy and ethics is the growing emphasis on inclusivity and diversity. While Wicca has always celebrated the balance of masculine and feminine energies, there is a growing recognition of the need to expand this inclusivity to encompass a wider range of identities and experiences. Many Wiccans are working to create more welcoming spaces for individuals of diverse backgrounds, genders, sexual orientations, and cultural heritages. This shift reflects a broader societal awareness of the importance of representation and inclusion in all aspects of life, including spirituality.

Inclusivity within Wicca goes beyond acknowledging diversity; it also involves a deep respect for the sacredness of all life and the interconnectedness of all beings. This perspective aligns with environmental ethics and the recognition that the well-being of the Earth and all its inhabitants is essential for a sustainable future. Many Wiccans are actively engaged in environmental activism, advocating for the protection of ecosystems, the responsible use of natural resources, and the reduction of environmental harm. This commitment to eco-spirituality reflects an evolving ethical perspective that emphasizes the importance of living in harmony with the Earth.

The future of Wiccan philosophy and ethics is also marked by a continued commitment to personal empowerment and ethical responsibility. Wiccans believe in the capacity of individuals to shape their own destinies, a perspective that encourages self-reflection and personal growth. This commitment to empowerment extends to ethical conduct, as Wiccans emphasize the importance of harmlessness, ethical magic, and responsible use of power. As the Wiccan community grows, it is likely that these principles will continue to guide individuals in their ethical decision-making and interactions with others.

Furthermore, the future of Wiccan ethics may see an increased focus on social justice and activism. Many Wiccans are already advocates for causes such as LGBTQ+ rights, racial equality, women's rights, and indigenous rights. This commitment to social justice aligns with Wicca's principles of inclusivity, diversity, and harmlessness. As the Wiccan community expands its influence and presence, it is likely that more Wiccans will engage in social justice activism and contribute to positive change on a broader societal level.

The evolving perspectives within Wiccan philosophy and ethics also intersect with the broader discourse on spirituality and religion in the modern world. As more individuals seek spiritual paths that resonate with their values and beliefs, there is a growing interest in earth-centered and nature-based traditions like Wicca. This trend suggests that the future of Wicca may involve increased visibility and acceptance in mainstream society, challenging misconceptions and stereotypes.

Ethical considerations related to teaching and sharing Wiccan knowledge are likely to continue to evolve in the future. Wiccans are committed to preserving the sacred mysteries of their tradition while also promoting transparency and accessibility. Striking a balance between secrecy and openness is an ongoing ethical challenge, and Wiccans will likely continue to explore ways to navigate this dilemma in a changing world where information is readily accessible.

The ethical dilemmas within the Wiccan community, such as secrecy, ethics of initiation, and conflicts, are also likely to evolve as the tradition continues to grow. Initiatory traditions may adapt to emphasize informed consent, autonomy, and ethical mentorship, addressing concerns about power dynamics and potential abuses. Conflict resolution processes and community-building practices may become more refined to ensure that ethical issues are promptly and constructively addressed.

In conclusion, the future of Wiccan philosophy and ethics is characterized by evolving perspectives that reflect the changing world and the growing diversity within the tradition. Inclusivity, eco-spirituality, personal empowerment, and a commitment to ethical responsibility are shaping the ethical landscape of Wicca. As the Wiccan community continues to expand and engage with contemporary ethical challenges, it will likely play a significant role in promoting inclusivity, social justice, and environmental sustainability. The evolving philosophy and ethics of Wicca demonstrate its resilience and adaptability, ensuring that it remains a vibrant and relevant spiritual path in the modern era.

Common challenges faced by Wiccans in a diverse world

Wicca, a contemporary pagan and witchcraft-based religion, has grown significantly since its emergence in the mid-20th century. As the Wiccan community continues to expand and interact with a diverse and complex world, its practitioners face a range of common challenges. In this section, we will explore some of the most prevalent challenges that Wiccans encounter in a diverse society, from misconceptions and stereotypes to issues related to religious freedom, discrimination, and community acceptance.

One of the most persistent challenges faced by Wiccans is the prevalence of misconceptions and stereotypes about their religion. Wicca has often been misrepresented in popular culture and media, leading to widespread misunderstandings. Common misconceptions include equating Wicca with Satanism, believing it to be solely focused on dark magic or curses, and associating it with secrecy and clandestine practices. These misconceptions can lead to prejudice, discrimination, and bias against Wiccans, as well as hinder their ability to practice their faith openly and without fear.

The challenge of religious freedom is another significant issue for Wiccans. While many countries protect the freedom of religion in their constitutions or legal frameworks, Wiccans continue to face instances of discrimination, intolerance, and exclusion. In some cases,

Wiccan rituals and practices have been met with resistance or hostility from individuals or groups who do not understand or respect the religion. This challenge underscores the importance of advocating for religious freedom and educating the public about the rights and beliefs of Wiccans and other minority religions.

Discrimination against Wiccans can take various forms, including workplace discrimination, denial of religious accommodations, and social exclusion. Some Wiccans have reported difficulties in finding employment or facing harassment at work due to their religious beliefs. Others have encountered challenges in accessing spiritual spaces, such as the denial of permission to use public venues for Wiccan rituals. Discrimination based on religious beliefs not only infringes on individuals' rights but also perpetuates the stigma and bias against Wicca within society.

Another challenge faced by Wiccans is the quest for acceptance and recognition within the broader religious and spiritual landscape. Wicca is still considered a relatively young religion in comparison to more established faiths. This can result in a lack of understanding or acknowledgment of Wiccan beliefs and practices by mainstream religious institutions. Wiccans often seek recognition and validation for their faith, hoping for equal treatment and representation in interfaith dialogues and religious discourse.
Interfaith relations present both challenges and opportunities for Wiccans. While many Wiccans are open to engaging in interfaith dialogues and building bridges with practitioners of other traditions, they may encounter resistance or skepticism from representatives of more established religions. Some individuals may be unwilling to acknowledge Wicca as a legitimate faith, which can hinder productive conversations and cooperation among diverse religious communities.

Inclusivity and diversity within the Wiccan community itself are areas that require attention and growth. While Wicca values the balance of masculine and feminine energies and promotes inclusivity, there is room for improvement in embracing a wider range of identities and experiences. The challenge lies in creating more welcoming spaces for individuals of diverse backgrounds, genders, sexual orientations, and cultural heritages within the Wiccan community. Achieving this inclusivity is essential for ensuring that Wicca remains a vibrant and relevant spiritual path in an increasingly diverse world.

The issue of cultural appropriation is another challenge that Wiccans must navigate. As a religion that draws on various spiritual and magical traditions, Wicca is often accused of appropriating elements from other cultures without proper respect or understanding. Ethical dilemmas related to cultural appropriation can arise when Wiccans integrate practices, symbols, or rituals from indigenous, African, or other non-European traditions into their own practice. Striking a balance between honoring the cultural origins of these practices and avoiding appropriation is a challenge that Wiccans face as they seek to create a respectful and inclusive spiritual path.

Additionally, the challenge of addressing internal conflicts and ethical dilemmas within the Wiccan community persists. Conflicts can arise from differences in beliefs, personalities, leadership styles, or interpretations of Wiccan teachings and ethics. These conflicts can be exacerbated by the often decentralized and autonomous nature of Wiccan practice. Resolving these issues and fostering a sense of unity and cooperation among practitioners requires a commitment to ethical conduct, open communication, and conflict resolution processes.

In conclusion, Wiccans face a range of common challenges in a diverse world, from misconceptions and stereotypes to issues related to religious freedom, discrimination, and community acceptance. These challenges highlight the importance of advocacy, education, and dialogue within and outside the Wiccan community. By addressing these challenges with resilience and integrity, Wiccans contribute to a more inclusive and tolerant society where individuals of all faiths can coexist harmoniously and practice their beliefs without fear of prejudice or discrimination.

Strategies for overcoming challenges and staying true to one's ethical principles

Wicca, a contemporary pagan and witchcraft-based religion, is guided by a set of ethical principles that emphasize harmlessness, personal responsibility, and respect for nature. However, like any spiritual path, Wicca presents its practitioners with various challenges that may test their commitment to these principles. In this section, we will explore strategies for overcoming challenges and staying true to one's ethical principles in Wicca, with a focus on maintaining personal integrity, fostering community support, engaging in open dialogue, and practicing mindfulness.

Personal integrity is foundational to navigating challenges while adhering to Wiccan ethical principles. Wiccans are encouraged to live authentically, with honesty and integrity in all aspects of their lives. When confronted with ethical dilemmas or difficult situations, practitioners can turn to their inner moral compass and core values to guide their decisions. By maintaining a strong sense of personal integrity, Wiccans can ensure that their actions align with their ethical principles, even in the face of external pressures or conflicts.

Fostering community support is another valuable strategy for overcoming challenges in Wicca. Wiccan practitioners often form or join covens or groups to share their spiritual journeys and support one another. In times of uncertainty or ethical dilemmas, the support and guidance of a community can provide valuable perspectives and insights. Discussing challenges openly with fellow Wiccans can lead to a deeper understanding of ethical principles and how they can be applied to specific situations. Furthermore, community support can help individuals feel more resilient and less isolated in the face of challenges.

Engaging in open dialogue is crucial for addressing and resolving ethical challenges in Wicca. Effective communication allows practitioners to share their perspectives, concerns, and questions with others in a respectful and constructive manner. When conflicts or ethical dilemmas arise, Wiccans should strive to engage in open and empathetic conversations with those involved. This approach can lead to a greater understanding of differing viewpoints, the identification of common ground, and the development of solutions that align with Wiccan ethical principles.

Practicing mindfulness is a fundamental strategy for staying true to one's ethical principles in Wicca. Mindfulness involves self-awareness, reflection, and a deep understanding of the consequences of one's actions. When faced with ethical dilemmas, practitioners can take the time to meditate, contemplate, and assess the potential outcomes of their choices. Mindfulness also encourages practitioners to consider the ethical implications of their actions from a broader perspective, such as their impact on the environment, other beings, and future generations.

Another valuable strategy for overcoming challenges in Wicca is the continuous study and exploration of the tradition's teachings and ethics. Wicca is a dynamic and evolving spiritual path that offers a wealth of resources for understanding its core principles. Practitioners can deepen their knowledge by reading books, attending workshops, and engaging in discussions with experienced Wiccans. A solid understanding of Wiccan ethics provides a solid foundation for making informed and ethical decisions in the face of challenges.

The practice of ritual and magic can also be a powerful strategy for overcoming challenges in Wicca. Rituals and spells can be tailored to address specific ethical dilemmas or personal obstacles. Through ritual work, Wiccans can focus their intention on finding solutions that are aligned with their ethical principles. Rituals can serve as a means of seeking guidance from the divine, fostering inner strength, and manifesting positive change in challenging situations.

It is important to note that overcoming challenges in Wicca does not always involve external actions or solutions. Sometimes, the most significant challenges are internal, such as doubts, fears, or conflicts within one's own beliefs or practices. In such cases, strategies like meditation, journaling, and seeking guidance from mentors or spiritual leaders can be valuable in exploring and resolving these inner conflicts while staying true to one's ethical principles.

In conclusion, staying true to one's ethical principles in Wicca requires a combination of personal integrity, community support, open dialogue, mindfulness, continuous study, and the use of ritual and magic. Challenges will inevitably arise on one's spiritual journey, but by employing these strategies, practitioners can navigate ethical dilemmas with authenticity and commitment. Ultimately, the pursuit of ethical excellence is a lifelong journey in Wicca, one that fosters personal growth, deepens spiritual understanding, and reinforces the core values that guide practitioners on their unique path within the tradition.

CONCLUSION

In conclusion, "Exploring Wiccan Ethics: Ethical Enchantments - Nurturing the Soul with Wiccan Philosophy and Ethical Practices" is an exploration of the rich and profound world of Wiccan spirituality and ethics. This ebook delves into the origins, core beliefs, and diverse traditions within Wicca, shedding light on the interconnectedness of all life and the sacredness of nature. It examines the role of deity and the God/Goddess, demonstrating how Wiccans forge a deep spiritual connection with the divine within the natural world.

The ebook delves into the significance of the Wheel of the Year, a sacred calendar that guides Wiccans through the seasons and rituals, emphasizing the eternal cycle of life, death, and rebirth. It explores the creation of sacred space and the importance of ethical considerations through the Wiccan Rede, promoting responsible and mindful living in harmony with the Earth.

Throughout its pages, this ebook seeks to unravel the mysteries of Wicca, offering insight into its historical development, diverse interpretations, and the profound impact it has on the lives of its practitioners. It recognizes Wicca as a modern spiritual path that draws inspiration from ancient traditions, fostering reverence for the natural world and a sense of interconnectedness with all life.

As readers embark on this journey through Wiccan philosophy and ethics, they will discover a path that encourages personal empowerment, ethical responsibility, and a deep connection with the Earth. It is a journey that invites reflection, mindfulness, and a renewed appreciation for the beauty and sacredness of the natural world.

In the realm of Wicca, the soul is nurtured through the embrace of ethical practices, the recognition of the divine within, and the celebration of the cycles of life and nature. "Exploring Wiccan Ethics: Ethical Enchantments" serves as a guide, offering both newcomers and seasoned practitioners an opportunity to explore and deepen their understanding of Wicca's spiritual richness and ethical wisdom. It is an invitation to embark on a path of enchantment, reverence, and ethical enlightenment, nurturing the soul in harmony with the profound philosophy and ethics of Wicca.

Thank you for buying and reading/ listening to our book. If you found this book useful/ helpful please take a few minutes and leave a review on the platform where you purchased our book. Your feedback matters greatly to us.

www.ingramcontent.com/pod-product-compliance
Lightning Source LLC
Chambersburg PA
CBHW052049150726
48002CB00002B/820